DEVELOPMENT CENTRE STUDIES

CONFLICT AND GROWTH IN AFRICA

Vol. 3: Southern Africa

By
Andrew Goudie *and* Bilin Neyapti

DEVELOPMENT CENTRE
OF THE ORGANISATION FOR ECONOMIC CO-OPERATION AND DEVELOPMENT

ORGANISATION FOR ECONOMIC CO-OPERATION AND DEVELOPMENT

Pursuant to Article 1 of the Convention signed in Paris on 14th December 1960, and which came into force on 30th September 1961, the Organisation for Economic Co-operation and Development (OECD) shall promote policies designed:

- to achieve the highest sustainable economic growth and employment and a rising standard of living in Member countries, while maintaining financial stability, and thus to contribute to the development of the world economy;
- to contribute to sound economic expansion in Member as well as non-member countries in the process of economic development; and
- to contribute to the expansion of world trade on a multilateral, non-discriminatory basis in accordance with international obligations.

The original Member countries of the OECD are Austria, Belgium, Canada, Denmark, France, Germany, Greece, Iceland, Ireland, Italy, Luxembourg, the Netherlands, Norway, Portugal, Spain, Sweden, Switzerland, Turkey, the United Kingdom and the United States. The following countries became Members subsequently through accession at the dates indicated hereafter: Japan (28th April 1964), Finland (28th January 1969), Australia (7th June 1971), New Zealand (29th May 1973), Mexico (18th May 1994), the Czech Republic (21st December 1995), Hungary (7th May 1996), Poland (22nd November 1996) and Korea (12th December 1996). The Commission of the European Communities takes part in the work of the OECD (Article 13 of the OECD Convention).

The Development Centre of the Organisation for Economic Co-operation and Development was established by decision of the OECD Council on 23rd October 1962 and comprises twenty-three Member countries of the OECD: Austria, Belgium, Canada, the Czech Republic, Denmark, Finland, France, Germany, Greece, Iceland, Ireland, Italy, Japan, Korea, Luxembourg, Mexico, the Netherlands, Norway, Poland, Portugal, Spain, Sweden and Switzerland, as well as Argentina and Brazil from March 1994, and Chile since November 1998. The Commission of the European Communities also takes part in the Centre's Advisory Board.

The purpose of the Centre is to bring together the knowledge and experience available in Member countries of both economic development and the formulation and execution of general economic policies; to adapt such knowledge and experience to the actual needs of countries or regions in the process of development and to put the results at the disposal of the countries by appropriate means.

The Centre has a special and autonomous position within the OECD which enables it to enjoy scientific independence in the execution of its task. Nevertheless, the Centre can draw upon the experience and knowledge available in the OECD in the development field.

338.96
C748
VOL.3

Publié en français sous le titre :

CONFLITS ET CROISSANCE EN AFRIQUE

Vol. 3 : Afrique australe

 THE OPINIONS EXPRESSED AND ARGUMENTS EMPLOYED IN THIS PUBLICATION ARE THE SOLE RESPONSIBILITY OF THE AUTHORS AND DO NOT NECESSARILY REFLECT THOSE OF THE OECD OR OF THE GOVERNMENTS OF ITS MEMBER COUNTRIES.

*
* *

Foreword

This publication is produced in the context of the Development Centre's work on seeking ways to integrate poorer countries into the world economy. It results specifically from the programme entitled "Political Economy and Development in Africa". Two other volumes complete the series.

Southern Africa – Mozambique, Malawi, Zambia, Zimbabwe and Botswana

The boundaries and names shown on this map do not imply official endorsement or acceptance by the OECD.

Table of Contents

Acknowledgements

The Development Centre would like to express its gratitude to the Government of Switzerland for the financial support given to the project on "Emerging Africa" in the context of which this study was carried out.

Preface

The seminar organised by the Development Centre in 1994 on growth prospects and the causes of economic stagnation in sub–Saharan Africa underlined the disastrous effects of the conflicts that have occurred in the region since the 1960s. Many economic failures in the region have been due to unrest and civil war. These conclusions led the Centre to undertake a project on the relationship between conflict and growth. This type of analysis is problematic as it calls upon disciplines far removed from economics; the ethnic, religious, linguistic, social and economic factors of conflict are so entangled that it is difficult to obtain a clear idea of the role of economic factors in order to suggest new economic policies liable to enhance the prevention of conflicts.

This book is an ambitious and courageous analysis, which examines five different countries, from war–torn Mozambique to peaceful and stable Botswana, over three decades. In the case of Mozambique, the authors show how internal factors of conflict mingled with those from outside, since RENAMO was supported, successively, by Rhodesia and South Africa. They also point out how the FRELIMO government also bears part of the responsibility through misguided socialist policies, the effects of which were compounded by RENAMO operations designed to ruin the economy. The human cost of this conflict was considerable as it resulted in the loss of hundreds of thousands of lives and provoked the displacement of millions of small farmers.

At the other end of the scale, Botswana has been able to draw the maximum amount of benefit from its diamond mines by reconciling growth with equity, attaining exceptional economic performance from which the entire population has been able to profit. Political stability in the country resulted from the absence of friction between ethnic or interest groups and from respect for the democratic process. Between these two extremes, Zimbabwe and Zambia (and Malawi to a lesser degree) represent cases of serious tensions and political instability due to ethnic conflict and interest–group rivalry. Minorities have used political power to misappropriate rents, rather than equitably distributing public expenditure.

From each country's history, the reader can begin to understand how political instability establishes itself within a country and interferes with sustained growth. This book describes all the factors in play: armed struggle (with conflict between movements as well as against non–democratic governments); dual socio–economic structures perpetuated after independence; inequality in asset distribution (land, fixed or human capital); injustice in the distribution of public services such as education and health; and the role of foreign actors, as in the case of Mozambique.

The authors' conclusions are of strong interest because they are based on a strict economic analysis of the causes of conflict. The authors find that respect for the democratic process, concern for equality and allowing a free market to develop represent the best means of ensuring the political stability needed so badly in these African societies.

Ulrich Hiemenz
Director
OECD Development Centre

September 1999

Executive Summary

Africa's disappointing development performance in recent decades has generally been associated with socio–political instability ranging from minor tension to extreme forms of conflict. To the extent that such instability creates uncertainty in the economic environment, it deters private investment and thus adversely affects development. Its sources should therefore be of primary concern in designing and implementing policies to achieve sustainable economic progress. This book provides a framework for the analysis of political and social instability, and uses it in five case studies — of Mozambique, Zimbabwe, Zambia, Botswana and Malawi — to identify the socio–economic determinants of political stability or instability in sub–Saharan Africa.

The Framework for Analysis

Socio–political instability runs from minor forms to extreme conflict in the form of civil and international war. This study puts its determinants into two main categories: *direct economic* ones, such as elements of economic policy or characteristics of the prevailing economic structure, and *non–economic or indirect economic* causes, primarily political, social or cultural in character although economic forces may drive them. The economic determinants receive the main emphasis, because they often have received relatively less attention in the analysis of conflict than political, diplomatic or military factors.

The potential for political instability generally relates directly to the division of interests that seek to affect wealth distribution. Country–specific characteristics that lead to the formation of such divisions therefore have great importance for the analysis of instability. The divisions evolve in connection with the distribution of resources or wealth. A distribution of assets either unfavourable for some social groups or perceived to be so enhances the potential for instability. "Assets" imply all sorts of income–generating elements, such as physical or human capital, financial assets, or simply access to or opportunities to benefit from government–owned assets.

Political instability usually arises with either an outbreak of accumulated discontent with the prevailing asset distribution or a distortion of that distribution. The former occurs in Africa in the increased destabilising potential of inequity between distinct social groupings, observed not only during the pre–colonial or colonial periods but also during post–colonial nationalisations. The latter results either from economic policies that impact social groups unevenly or are perceived to do so, or from external economic distortions. Domestic economic policies of particular significance include fiscal, land reform and structural policies, all with distributional implications. Fluctuations in international commodity prices, environmental and climatic transformations, and economic pressures in neighbouring economies exemplify external economic distortions. The response of government to these underlying sources of destabilisation is a prominent concern of this book. Depending on their net socio–political costs, responses may range from meeting the claims of the dissenters to rejecting them, possibly with repression.

The non–economic sources of political instability include specifically the opportunities for political expression, the status of human rights and quality of law enforcement, and discrimination against identifiable social groupings. Looking at ethnic structure, often the most convenient basis for classifying social groupings, is especially important, not least to guard against a confusion between ethnic and fundamentally economic or political elements. With the end of the Cold War and the start of the democratisation process since the late 1980s, intra–state conflict has gradually replaced inter–state conflict in Africa. As this has unfolded, ethnic identification has appeared as a strong basis for forming new pressure groups that wish to influence state structures. Emerging political parties have frequently targeted ethnic groupings to enhance political support, especially where ethnic groupings clearly overlap geographic areas and occupational groupings. Such tendencies towards ethnic polarisation may pave the way to ethnic–based discrimination and instability, even if the origins of such instability are primarily economic or political.

Case Studies

The approach adopted here explicitly acknowledges that socio–political instability has highly economy–specific roots. Case studies, nevertheless, reveal many complementary elements and lead to some common insights that help to explain the wide spectrum of socio–political outcomes within the same geographical region.

Mozambique

An armed struggle between the government (FRELIMO) and opposition resistance forces (RENAMO) dominated the post–independence period in Mozambique, severely disrupting social and economic life. RENAMO mainly targeted economic establishments, making the cost of the conflict immense in terms of both massive population displacement and the destruction of production and distribution networks. Floods, droughts and the exodus of Portuguese settlers during 1974–76 further exacerbated the decline in economic activity.

It is surprisingly difficult to identify any domestic political basis for this turmoil, which led to such high human and material costs until the Peace Agreement in 1992. Regional political factors, however, have much to offer in identifying sources of the seemingly internal conflict. The resistance forces first organised in Southern Rhodesia, in collaboration with former colonial elements that left Mozambique and then re–established themselves in South Africa. The Rhodesian interests supporting RENAMO monitored the Zimbabwe People's Army, which conducted activities in Mozambique; the Portuguese interests simply destabilised the country. The radical ideological stance of the FRELIMO government and its attitude towards white minority governments provoked ideological and financial support for RENAMO from non–communist countries. In addition to these political sources of instability, the economic claims of previous settlers seeking to regain political power and economic mismanagement by the FRELIMO government were domestic economic factors that contributed to political instability.

Although economic policy had a modest role during the internal conflict, it played a key part during the restoration of socio–political stability which followed a period of increased repression of dissent. Both international financing and appropriate economic policy, targeted primarily to strengthen governance and promote economic and social stabilisation, restoration of rural life and sustainable economic growth, supported disarmament, demobilisation, reintegration and resettlement.

Zimbabwe

In Zimbabwe, conflict approached the dimensions of civil war after independence. Colonial rule had established large estates on the most productive lands, exclusively owned by Europeans, whereas Africans did subsistence farming on lower–grade communal lands. After the Unilateral Declaration of Independence in 1965 and until a major political transformation with the first multi–party elections in 1980, Africans remained severely deprived of economic advancement and political participation.

Even as Africans suffered discrimination as a group, they remained deeply divided among themselves by ethnic affiliations, which severely protracted the instability. The two largest ethnic groups, *Shona* and *Ndebele*, trained and armed by different international sources, competed for power and divided politically along ethnic lines. Meanwhile, South Africa constituted an external destabilising factor as it wished to maintain Zimbabwe's economic and political dependence. Hence, conflict between the two groups continued until after the unification between their representative political parties to form a new government in 1987, with a commitment to maintain a single–party system.

After 1980, the government kept the economic and institutional structures mainly unchanged, although incorporating African elements into them. The expanding African *petite bourgeoisie* rapidly came to associate itself with the white commercial farming and industrial interests that favoured prevailing mechanisms of allocation and distribution. As the state sector expanded markedly, however, its rapid Africanisation in a highly controlled economy offered a convenient environment for rent seeking. When the stabilising elements of government policy, such as increased social spending in the early 1980s, proved unsustainable, the government chose to maintain many repressive elements of the previous regime.

Repressive policies, however, further provoked the potential for unrest. Important degrees of distrust and resentment persist between indigenous and non–indigenous groups, the latter having privileged positions in trade; between *Shona* and the minority ethnic groups; between the political elite and rest of the African community; and, within the government, between rent seekers and those with market–oriented attitudes. In general, minority ethnic groups feel marginalised both politically and economically.

Zambia

Zambia obtained its independence against the colonial will to maintain the Central African Federation, the bulk of whose resources came from Zambia's rich copper revenues. The colonial emphasis on copper production progressively empowered union labour, which became well organised and played a large role not only in the independence movement but also in socio–economic policies after independence.

Organised interests evolved after independence, however. The trade unions competed increasingly with the emergent political and bureaucratic elite and urban groups, changing the locus of conflict from Africans versus whites towards a clash between narrow African interest groups and national objectives. The official reaction to the demands of powerful unions was sometimes accommodating and sometimes repressive, mirrored in recurring social unrest and two switches of political regime — to a one–party system in 1973 and back to a multi–party system in 1991. The decline of copper revenues greatly influenced the first transition, as it severely restrained the accommodative potential of the government. The lack of economic diversification further exacerbated the impact of exogenous shocks. Moreover, rapid Africanisation of the state and the economy, without sufficient training and experience, aggravated socio–economic problems and thus increased the potential for political instability. The government's repressive policies and degenerating economic performance both contributed to increased political instability, leading finally to democratic transition in 1991. That shift, notwithstanding that repressive policies subsided only slowly, raised the potential for political stability. The implementation of economic reforms became an easier task because the suffering of socio–economic groups had become more widespread under the economic and political mismanagement of the 1980s.

Botswana

Botswana enjoyed political stability after independence because it experienced a favourable economic shock and had a government which pursued sensible and equitable policies. The discovery of diamond mines led to an unmatched growth performance, enabling the government to undertake many social projects. Moreover, Botswana historically had a quite low potential for political instability, with a democratic tradition and no major narrow interest groups with distinct means of expression. Convinced that Botswana had no major natural resources, the colonial regime did not pursue major economic rents and its governance did not lead to the organisation of narrow economic interest groups among the *Batswana*. This and the lack of ethnic–based associations facilitated the later implementation of equitable policies without political opposition, which in turn let a politically stable environment thrive.

Malawi

One of the poorest countries in the world, Malawi did not attract much foreign investment during the colonial period as it too had few national resources. Although it benefited from trade relations as the only western–aligned country in the region, economic downturn after the late 1970s revealed the weaknesses in the economy, namely a lack of diversification, dependence on primary–commodity exports and the governing party's dominant economic role. Although encouraged, development of the private sector remained linked with the state through political loyalties.

Malawi's apparent political stability after independence nevertheless persisted for a long time under effective mechanisms of far–reaching political control and a relatively well–managed state. Political measures largely repressed the emergence of interest groups and an effective political opposition. In time, however, increasing poverty and inequalities provoked by unfavourable economic developments led eventually to an increased potential for political instability. A democratic transition finally took place in 1994 after growing expression of both domestic and external opposition to the government's repressive measures.

Some Observations

Several common elements of political instability emerge from the country studies. Culture and history have vast implications for the achievement and maintenance of political stability. Countries with histories of armed struggle, within groups or against the colonial power, appear prone to relatively higher degrees of political instability than those lacking such histories; conversely, countries with relatively peaceful histories have generally attained more stability than others. The dual socio–economic structures generated during the colonial period and maintained thereafter, coupled with the formation and strengthening of socio–economic interest groups within those structures, particularly affect asset distribution and thus have a potentially great impact on the degree of political instability. The emergence and political power of such narrow interest groups generally relate directly to the coincidence of ethnic groupings with distinct occupations and regions.

Exogenous elements, such as the international political and economic setting and the natural endowments of a country, play a large role because they are closely connected with growth potential and thus with the ability of the government to prevent dissent through redistribution. Finally, good economic management enables a sustainable balance between the objectives of growth and equity that minimises the potential for the emergence of political instability. All the case studies, moreover, strongly suggest that democratic mechanisms and market institutions are crucial for successfully implementing policies to achieve sustainable economic development and political stability.

Chapter 1

An Approach to the Analysis of Conflict

The Framework for Analysis

Economic development in Africa has undoubtedly not met expectations in recent decades, not only in comparison with other LDCs but also from an absolute perspective: real per capita incomes have dropped in many African economies[1]. The continent also has seen major political and social instability, ranging from relatively minor manifestations — although in excess of widely accepted norms of political opposition — to extreme conflict in the form of civil and international war. While it is inappropriate to imply any direct and simple causality between instability and economic performance, given the multiplicity of determinants apparently instrumental in shaping socio–political tension, a strong *prima facie* case exists for identifying such tension and conflict as a major determinant of the prevailing economic environment and the process of economic development. Kanbur (1995) notes that, without the restoration of peace in African situations where order has broken down through civil war or social unrest, no development can occur. Moreover, development has shown considerable volatility, with many apparent advances periodically reversed or only poorly sustained over the medium to long term. The onset of socio–political tensions appears at first sight to have played an important role in this volatility and, perhaps unlike many other determining factors, to have the potential to cause catastrophic reversals rather than more marginal impacts. This alone suggests that its role may be pivotal for sustainable development.

If the primary objective of policy is to achieve sustainable and relatively stable development, and if the establishment and maintenance of an appropriately enabling economic environment represents a critical factor in securing that objective[2], then the manner in which socio–political instability creates uncertainty in the economic environment should be a primary concern. Such uncertainty has particular importance given the central role in development of the private sector in general and of private

15

investment in particular. Private foreign investment will likely be especially sensitive to uncertainty. Over the long term, attracting such resources has major significance for development.

This chapter seeks to provide a framework within which policy–makers may consider the economic determinants of socio–political instability — elements of economic policy or characteristics of the prevailing economic structure — and thus identify primary areas for reconsideration of policy. Economic factors will necessarily vary in importance *vis–à–vis* non–economic ones, depending on the specific characteristics of national economies. While the main focus here rests on the economic elements, a broader view does at times enter to provide the necessary balance. Indeed, many factors which appear to be political, cultural or social rather than economic may themselves be driven by economic forces. It is as necessary to capture these indirect economic determinants as the more direct ones.

The approach explicitly acknowledges that instability is highly economy–specific in its underlying roots. This necessitates considerable caution in the interpretation of and response to a single period of instability in a given economy. One must assume that policy management to achieve improved, sustainable socio–political stability will be equally differentiated, although episodes in one country can have relevance in similar situations elsewhere.

The Primary Economic Sources of Instability

From an economic perspective, the potential for discontent and tension leading to the outbreak of conflict may arise whenever any group in society perceives the distribution of economic assets as unacceptable. The relevant society must be defined to incorporate both resident nationals and nationals abroad who retain an interest in the affairs of the domestic state. This broad definition is especially important where substantial numbers of people live in either voluntary or forced exile. The Rwanda conflict since 1959 provides an example; at various times, considerable numbers of refugees dwelled in neighbouring countries, notably Uganda and Zaire. Discontent may emerge and evolve dynamically in two primary ways:

a) the actual distribution of economic assets moves unfavourably from the perspective of one or more groups; or

b) despite little or even no substantive change in distributional patterns, group *perceptions* of them shift unfavourably.

The two key questions then practically pose themselves. What generates real changes in the pattern of asset distribution and thereby provokes discontent? What factors govern the transformation of perceptions through time? The greatest interest centres on situations in which both the real distributional patterns undergo significant changes and changing perceptions accompany them. Here, the two forces would interact and reinforce pressures within the society; if a propensity for socio–political instability exists, tensions would arise.

The initial pattern of asset distribution may be a long–standing source of major instability, attributable to historical events that occurred decades or even centuries earlier. If so, current tensions may not result from any recent change in the pattern of distribution or in perceptions of it. Both may be clearly established, long–standing and relatively static, requiring a long–term historical analysis to understand them.

New or emerging tension, however, has more recent causes. Real asset distribution may change, perhaps substantially, in response to a specific big event or, less strikingly, as part of a more gradual trend that progressively erodes a previously established norm. Similarly, some government policies, e.g. nationalisation or land–reform programmes, may impact the stock of assets profoundly, while other elements of economic policy may affect resource allocation only at the margin. The discovery of major mineral resources has often had the potential greatly to disturb the previous equilibrium. In Botswana, the diamond discoveries of the late 1960s did so, but with a good result: socio–political stability was largely maintained. In contrast, the mineral discoveries in Nigeria and Angola arguably increased the potential for conflict. In general, then, the economic sources of instability that might affect real distributional patterns can take two forms:

a)   present and prospective economic policies and the expectations that they generate for future patterns of asset distribution; and/or

b)   exogenous economic forces, typically emanating from international markets, environmental change or actions of foreign governments.

As noted above, discontent also could result from evolving perceptions which do not reflect any substantive redistribution. This process is shaped in part by factors affecting a group's appreciation of its relative standing within society, which can transform expectations, often dramatically, through many mechanisms. They include political transformation, the termination of conflict or, more indirectly, perhaps even the extension of educational opportunities. Historical legacies will certainly play a major role. A long–standing, gross inequity, for example, has more likelihood of provoking reaction as a group's awareness of its relative standing in the social structure grows and moves it towards a rejection of the *status quo*. In some economies, an enhanced perception of absolute deprivation may increase tension and instability; greater awareness of quantitative and/or qualitative deficiencies in the standard of living, rather than stimulation by reference groups or comparative standards, may lead to growing discontent. The poorest groups, however, typically lack the organisational capacity to display serious dissent. The strength of these factors will no doubt differ between societies and over time, but understanding their role in the determination of instability is important to the definition of appropriate measures to prevent discontent from being transformed into more serious forms of instability and conflict.

The Equilibrium of Economic Resource Allocation

One can assert as a basic hypothesis that, to the extent that the prevailing distribution of economic assets becomes unacceptable to a part of the population, the system will be in disequilibrium and potential will exist for increasing levels of dissent and tension that may ultimately lead to more serious outbreaks of conflict and violence. "Equilibrium" does not imply the agreement of all social groups with the pattern of asset distribution, but does entail its broad acceptance and the absence of a major challenge or the threat of such a challenge, through non–constitutional and, especially, violent mechanisms. In contrast, "disequilibrium" would connote the threat or reality of such a challenge.

The economic resources or assets involved require definition in the broadest sense and from the perspective of the individual or interest group central to the particular circumstance of instability. They should include all elements that generate real and imputed incomes. Their range should encompass all resources or assets over which the individual or group has established but differing rights. These may be strictly personal assets, with clearly defined legal rights attached to them, or social assets derived from state or communal ones, in which the individual has no property claims but only rights founded on custom, use or established access:

a)   capital assets, as traditionally defined to include land, domestic capital, productive capital, natural resources and accumulated stocks of production;

b)   human capital, derived from education and skills acquired over time;

c)   financial assets;

d)   access to and opportunities to benefit from the services provided by government–owned assets, ranging from social services (education, health, water and sanitation) to services of the economic infrastructure (transportation and telecommunications). The more segmented a society becomes in this respect, and the more this is perceived, the greater the potential for tension. Such segmentation may result from design, inadvertently from long–established policies and from physical and geographical barriers, prohibitive cost structures, administrative obstacles or discrimination[3]. It also can appear in variations in the quality of service delivery, which can be marked; and *e)* access to, and opportunities to benefit from, employment in general and specific employment opportunities. This includes access to both official and unofficial sources of employment and income–generating opportunities. The distribution of rents will play a major role, as will the prevailing entry barriers.

The Typology of Instability

Not all kinds of discord and dispute necessarily signal instability, Some forms of conflict may be natural and desirable elements of development, if they occur in institutional settings that prevent disagreement from spilling over into violence. Dissent through normal, constitutional channels is not here considered as instability, although it can of course play a role in stimulating other forms of dissent that should properly be considered as promoting instability. Equally, the expression of dissent through the accepted mechanisms of free speech — e.g. the media or *ad hoc* processes of consultation or negotiation within normal constitutional structures — is not *per se* identifiable as instability. One may also discount individual acts of dissent if, as typically, they cannot destabilise society as a whole. While one dissenter or a small number of them may accurately reflect the intense opposition of a considerably larger group, the dissent does not effectively constitute a threat or have the power to destabilise unless the group, or a substantial part of it, expresses reasonably coherent opposition.

Nevertheless, instability does embrace a wide range of situations[4]:

a) *minor instability* includes non–violent group action through demonstrations, mass strikes or mass civil disobedience. It may have the potential to develop into a more serious state;

b) *major instability* occurs when group activity incorporates violent conflict, but stops short of systematically taking up arms. It may range from violent demonstrations and riots to *ad hoc* attacks on property and people, but does not entail a structured, armed struggle; and

c) *civil war*, the most severe form, involves the systematic use of armed force in pursuit of a cause.

The nature of instability will vary not only in relation to the seriousness of the issues as perceived by dissenting groups, but also according to their opportunity to display one or another of its forms. For example, urban groupings will typically find greater opportunities for major instability, and more to gain from it, than will rural groupings. Yet the strength of dissent in a rural context may be equally severe even if major instability is absent. Here, dissent may find expression through civil disobedience and, at the extreme, the virtual refusal to comply with the law of central and local

Government by, for instance, refusing to pay taxes. Such dissent might well get classified as "minor instability", but it has many features that in other circumstances might lead to major instability.

The period over which dissent is displayed affects its potential to have major repercussions on the broader economic environment. Short, isolated outbursts, even of major instability and although important to those immediately involved, probably will have negligible significance for the national economy if their repetition is not expected. As their frequency increases, and as expectations of prolonged instability rise, they take on a more insidious form with considerably more serious implications for the society and economy. Moreover, and in reality, situations of relatively minor initial instability may well degenerate over time into progressively more serious forms with far more disruptive effects.

The Sources of Economic Asset Disequilibrium

The Prevailing Distribution of Economic Assets

If, in a given economy, the prevailing distribution pattern functions as a long-standing source of disequilibrium, it may be static, with little real change over a protracted period, but unstable because unaccepted and challenged by important groups within society. The two aspects of such situations which merit analysis involve the definition of property rights and the acceptability of the distribution pattern itself.

The Definition of Property Rights

In many situations, and irrespective of the appropriateness or otherwise of the distribution pattern, the inherited structure of property rights may be neither satisfactorily defined nor accepted as having an appropriate legal foundation by society as a whole. This state of affairs could have arisen under several possible circumstances.

Incompatible Legal Codes. First, and probably most important, clashing legal codes may claim the loyalties of different social groups. Examples exist where people may refer to effectively three codes: traditional law, colonial law and the post-Independence legal system[5]. Even where the codes may not be strictly incompatible, with later codes having legally supplanted earlier ones, different groups may continue to consider that earlier codes remain in force and refuse to acknowledge the prevailing legal system and structure as having precedence. This problem appears most starkly in economies that have undergone more dramatic and less orderly constitutional transformation, as in coups or revolutions. Land assets probably provide the best example of unresolved property rights in the aftermath of a civil war or coup, especially when major groups become exiled when the event overthrows previously established property rights.

The Assumption of Ownership by Government. The government may earlier have expropriated economic assets on terms and conditions not accepted at the time by all the parties involved and still subject to dispute and challenge. In other situations, government may have assumed effective ownership of economic assets abandoned by their original owners during war or mass migration, as, for example, in post–colonial Angola and Mozambique. In these instances, legal rights may simply not have been established at all. The concept of asset ownership, therefore, is often far from transparent and this in itself represents an important potential source of social and political tension and instability.

The Cession of Property Rights. A ruling government may have attempted formally to impose deadlines on original owners for the repossession of previously abandoned economic assets, prior to the assumption of state ownership and perhaps later redistribution of the assets to others. The original owners may well perceive as unjust such unilateral attempts to restore order to the structure of property rights, notably when an exiled community still considers return to the homeland as too dangerous or otherwise imprudent, thus failing to observe the deadline and losing its property rights in the eyes of the regime. Because the legal legitimacy of the official action remains subject to challenge, such situations closely relate to those described in the first category above.

The Certainty of Rights. Having a single legal code that defines property rights does not suffice; certainty of its implementation and enforcement by the judiciary must accompany it. Lack of adherence to accepted rights would be as damaging as their absence, inevitably providing a source of tension.

The Acceptability of the Prevailing Distribution of Economic Assets

In many instances, and notwithstanding that judicial judgements on asset ownership are uncontested, one or more groups may perceive the prevailing distribution itself as inequitable. The historical origins of this discontent may date back many decades, and may be associated with economic actions which established a social structure whose distribution of both political and economic powers became unacceptable to the disaffected group or groups. Several African examples have obvious relevance.

The Pre–Colonial Legacy. Long–established social structures in many countries reflect inequities in asset distribution that clearly have destabilising potential. They exist, for example, in historical patterns of land settlement, in the polarisation of

21

sedentary and nomadic peoples, or in farming and herding traditions. They find reflection in the Hutu–Tutsi disputes of Burundi and Rwanda, in the Tuareg unrest of Mali or, at the extreme, under the system of apartheid established by statute in South Africa. Each social system, with or without the assent of all affected interests, bore an implied, *de facto* pattern of asset distribution.

The Colonial Legacy. Many colonial systems incorporated discrimination against certain social groups that established major inequities in asset distribution. Differently but with similar effect, discriminatory exclusion from education under colonial rule not only created an immediate source of discontent but also, perhaps more importantly, implanted a long–term bias against the underprivileged. This effectively excluded them for many generations from the most lucrative income–generating opportunities.

The Role of State Ownership. The legitimacy of previous state actions to nationalise land or other assets may not be contested. Nonetheless, considerable opposition to these processes may persist if dissenters consider them to have greatly disadvantaged certain social groupings *vis–à–vis* others, especially when the ruling government appears to have favoured its constituency.

Disturbances in Economic Asset Equilibrium

Macroeconomic Linkages between Economic Growth, Policy Reform and Instability. The repercussions of socio–political instability on economic development have been extensively researched[6]. While the early work of Hibbs (1973) determined that socio–political instability did not impact on economic growth, later studies have found that it has significant adverse repercussions on both investment and growth[7]. In general, a strong presumption exists that instability will create an economic environment in which the perception of high risk and uncertainty deters private–sector investment and thus constrains the rate of development. Similarly, economic reform typically becomes more difficult in the face of intense and potentially disruptive opposition, which forces the adoption and implementation of slower adjustment paths. The converse also is broadly accepted: a stable socio–political climate will stimulate development, both promoting private–sector activity and facilitating more rapid economic adjustment programmes.

The nature of the reverse linkage — how growth and economic reform programmes impact on socio–political instability — is more enigmatic. Two questions have particular relevance. First, does economic growth uniformly and universally lead to reduced levels of socio–political tension and to the reduction of the threat of conflict? Second, how do economic adjustment programmes affect the propensity for tension and conflict to occur? Two alternative mechanisms linking growth to stability (or instability) have operated in different economies at different times.

Mutually Reinforcing Low Growth and Instability. In a stagnant or contracting economy, one would expect any susceptibility to instability to be more critical than in an expanding economy. This arguably happened in Zambia after 1975, for example, following the collapse of copper revenues. The scenario will likely produce an insidious vicious circle, in which deteriorating socio–political conditions tend to exacerbate the original stagnation and further deter private–sector development. Breaking the cycle becomes exceptionally difficult; the declining economy fails to provide means for the government to finance any major programmes to reduce instability, while the instability dampens private–sector incentives at a time when the public sector is highly constrained.

The Sustainable Development Path. In an expanding economy, by contrast, one would expect *ceteris paribus* that instability could be more readily controlled and indeed ameliorated. Botswana's diamond boom of the 1970s and 1980s facilitated growth and development that kept forces for instability in check. This sort of outcome depends critically on several underlying assumptions. First, when economic growth raises living standards, the gains must at the very least be uniformly spread through the society or, more probably, benefit social groups with the most marked potential for discontent. Second, the gains must be sufficiently significant to compensate for other grievances that the group in question perceives. Third, because getting growth started must necessarily constitute the first step, the prior question arises whether this can in fact be achieved without immediately exacerbating tensions; this issue is considered further below. Huntington (1968) has argued that growth, once achieved, may actually aggravate instability if it generates expectations that cannot be fulfilled as rapidly as desired. It might even generate new sources of tension.

Instability and Economic Reform

Economic policy design varies considerably across Africa, as does the degree to which economic reform has taken place over recent years, but most countries' need to pursue further reforms is uncontested. The nature of that reform process is hotly disputed, notably between aid communities and governments, but not the basic requirement for adjustment. Some have argued that, while growth can in principle contribute substantively to conflict prevention, the mechanisms for establishing sustainable growth — typically programmes of macroeconomic and structural adjustment — are themselves highly divisive and stimulate instability. The virtuous circle of increased growth, greater stability and further development can indeed become sustainable, but the role of economic reform is more controversial.

Given most economies' need for external assistance to meet continuing debt and external payment difficulties, and the clear stance of the donor community on reforms, governments often see few alternatives to adjustment programmes in order to gain the critical financial resources. This raises important questions of how feasible adjustment really is in situations of serious socio–political instability, and how much the adjustment process itself may exacerbate or alleviate instability. Any of three approaches to adjustment may apply at different times to different economies.

The Basic Approach. The fundamental rationale articulated by the multilateral financial institutions for economic adjustment in most African economies is extensively documented[8]. Many African observers and non–governmental organisations (NGOs)[9] have highlighted the controversial elements of this approach. In the 1980s it provoked hostility for seeming to accord primacy to macroeconomic adjustment and to internationally oriented and market–based economic structures over the redistributional goals of economic management. In essence, these arguments assert that the approach disregards the complexities of individual economies, notably the implications for instability and equity, and substantively increases the risk of intensified instability. In contrast, its advocates would argue that, without its stress on basic principles, other efforts to promote development and distributional equity will fail. They assume broadly that this approach will generate economic processes which benefit all of society, over time, to a far greater extent than predominantly distributional policies alone could achieve.

The Contextual Approach. The second approach is a variant of the first; indeed, some observers have exaggerated their differences. It sees economic reform as a prerequisite for sustainable growth and thus one of the primary elements of policy — but emphasises the imperative of designing reforms to the very precise economic and social circumstances of a country in order not to stimulate instability that could undermine reform, and not to weaken progress towards the elimination of poverty. It may, for example, entail enhanced distribution policies and slower macroeconomic adjustment[10]. One could view it as gradualist, because it explicitly takes into account constraints which tend to slow the reform process; but this implies the existence of a trade–off. In practice, some would argue that few or no alternatives exist, if adjustment is not to meet with substantive opposition and founder; any trade–off, therefore, may obtain only in the very short term, before opposition to the programme mounts.

The Deep Crisis Approach. This view accepts that the threat of instability jeopardises the successful implementation of essential economic reform programmes and the establishment of sustainable growth. It also acknowledges the importance of an appropriate political consensus to sustain a programme beyond the initial phase. From this perspective, it argues that, to avoid the anticipated instability, economic reform should be timed explicitly to coincide with periods of major internal crisis, when the scope for dissent may have drastically weakened. Such crises may come exogenously, as with droughts or other major climatic disasters[11], or embody the accumulated results of economic and financial mismanagement. In both instances, major policy changes may paradoxically become more feasible politically, particularly if the pressures for action on sensitive issues can be attributed to external forces. Many would argue that the policy steps taken at such a time should be not gradualist but substantial, to show serious and long–term intent, a signal of irreversibility in the adjustment process as important as the timing of the programme. From this perspective, reform does not provoke instability because of its opportunistic implementation.

The Combined Impact of Growth and Economic Reform on Instability

The possibility, introduced above, of a trade–off between the pace of economic reform and instability implies the prospect of higher long–term growth if instability is carefully monitored and taken into account in economic reform policy. The prospect is by no means a self–evident certainty; the relevant economic inter–relationships are complex, uncertain and highly dependent on the economy in question. The fundamental issue concerns whether a deceleration of the rate of economic reform and a similar slowing of economic growth in the short to medium term are the necessary prices of reduced instability and tension and the prospect of higher long–term growth.

This raises three further questions. First, are more equitable explicit or implicit distributional policies necessary for reduced instability? Do they constitute a prerequisite, even assuming that they are unlikely to be sufficient? Second, do slower growth and more protracted reform come as the inevitable price of greater equity and improvement in the distribution of economic resources? Third, will not slower reform and growth themselves become instrumental in exacerbating instability over the longer term, notwithstanding the short–term benefit from reduced instability?

The World Bank (1989) strongly asserts that equitable growth is necessary as "a precondition both for political stability and ultimately for sustained growth". Certainly, instances will occur where the redirection of government investment expenditure towards equity objectives may reduce short–term growth; higher educational expenditures present an example, as investments in human capital whose returns would typically lag the outlays[12]. Even in this example, however, the issue could be interpreted as one of short–run versus long–run growth, rather than of growth versus distribution. Most writers have observed a relatively robust relationship between initial degrees of income equality and subsequent economic growth rates[13].

The potential for a trade–off between stability and growth remains unclear. The ultimate impact of the two central policy alternatives — maintaining an economic reform programme without specific measures to cater to claims for redistributive policy, or adjusting the reform programme to accommodate such claims — will always be theoretically indeterminate. If economic reforms that establish higher growth rates tend to reduce instability and favour continuing economic growth, while the absence of distributional measures tends to exacerbate instability and discourage development, then the net impact on instability and longer–term growth will be uncertain *a priori*. Conversely, the same indeterminacy holds if a distributional policy tends to reduce instability and thereby encourage development, while slower reform and the lower growth that may be associated with it tend to aggravate instability and deter longer-term growth.

Even more fundamentally, can the implementation of an economic reform programme indeed be viable in the presence of serious instability? Many would argue that no option exists to reject a serious, potentially destabilising political claim outright and pursue an economic policy independently of it. Once again, the degree of instability becomes important; relatively minor discontent may be tolerated and not prove significant enough to impinge on a government programme, but more substantial unrest might well compel a reappraisal of policy. Certainly, it is hard to envisage the development of private–sector interests on any significant scale in the presence of substantial instability and with the perceived threat of its deterioration. This suggests that growth could not be long sustained in such circumstances, and that a stable social and political environment is a prerequisite for a stable economic one.

The Specific Elements of Economic Policy

This chapter has made many general references to economic policy, with no consideration of specific policy instruments. In many respects this is appropriate, because the diversity of experience amongst economies makes generalisation problematic. Nonetheless, it is useful to distinguish several relevant fields of economic policy because they impact differentially on identifiable social groupings.

Some policies have implications for the equilibrium of the pattern of asset distribution. The analysis so far has made a strong assumption, which remains to be tested rigorously, that such policies do have the capacity to ameliorate or augment instability through their effects on the asset–distribution equilibrium. In the presence of a prevailing equilibrium, however, a range of distributions around the *status quo* may exist, within which adverse distributional policy would not generate instability and would be tolerated. Equally, disequilibrium conditions may contain a range within which instability cannot be diffused. How substantial a distributional policy would be required in any given circumstance to transform the present pattern sufficiently to move it outside this equilibrium range in the first case, or within the range in the second? Much depends on the relative significance of the policy as a determinant of instability, given the multiplicity of relevant factors. One can delineate several potentially significant policy areas[14].

a) *Fiscal Policy with Explicit Distributional Objectives* encompasses a range of public expenditure decisions with a direct impact on distinct social groupings, or a regional subsidisation element, when it provides to a group or region government services with a value exceeding fiscal revenues from the group or region[15]. It incorporates:

i) the redirection of investment, especially to provide social services (education, health, water and sewerage) and economic infrastructure (notably transportation), given their high visibility, immediate impact and direct contribution to living standards; and

ii) income redistribution, through either the tax/transfer system or the direct distribution of consumer goods.

b) *The Transfer of Existing Resources* includes land–reform policies in particular, but they are likely to be relatively divisive and have the potential both to create additional instability and to spread that already prevailing.

c) *Structural Policy with Implicit Distributional Implications.* Many structural reform measures can either enhance or detract from prevailing equity patterns; such effects typically have only secondary importance in policy design. One of the clearest examples arises in reforms which suppress centralised, administrative control over resource distribution in favour of market–based systems, especially those responsive to international price signals. Adopted on economic efficiency grounds, such reforms will entail simultaneous repercussions on distribution when they affect the allocation of foreign exchange, consumer prices, nominal interest rates and the like. They will create winners and losers among specific groups within the economy.

Some of these policy areas have the potential not only to alter relative distributional patterns but also to change groups' absolute living standards. Moreover, one should not overlook the distributional effects of either macroeconomic policies not explicitly aimed at any distributional change, or policies to improve governance and accountability and to reduce corruption.

Exogenous Economic Sources of Instability

Internal stability in some economies clearly lies vulnerable to external forces over which domestic governments have little if any direct control[16]. Several such forces can impact very rapidly on the domestic asset distribution pattern.

a) *Volatile and Unanticipated Fluctuations in World Market Prices*, particularly when they affect specific sectors. These impacts typically get magnified in economies with extremely high concentrations of production in such sectors. The collapse of the copper price in Zambia provides a classic example; copper production accounted for around 40 per cent of GDP and 90 per cent of export revenues before 1975, and the loss of the revenues severely exacerbated existing tensions between the government and the increasingly powerful union movement.

b) *Environmental and Climatic Changes.* Many regions of Africa have felt such changes, either through the loss or depletion of a resource, or with the exploitation of previously unknown or untapped natural resources. In some Sahelian economies, desertification and the progressive loss of grazing or agricultural lands not only bears on current production, but also — far more importantly in the long term — impacts on fundamental social structures by forcing groups to amend their traditional lifestyles and preferred production methods; patterns of asset distribution long considered broadly acceptable get called into question by group reactions to these external pressures. Conversely, the discovery of new resources, as in Nigeria or Angola, can transform the pattern of natural resource distribution within a country.

c) *Economic Pressures in Neighbouring Economies* can produce significant secondary effects from the policy programmes they adopt. For example, governments at various times have introduced policy initiatives to repatriate expatriate workers, as in the case of miners working in South Africa. The economies to which the workers return often have faced serious losses of foreign remittances, the mainstay of local communities. Moreover, an influx of unemployed individuals, often young men accustomed to relatively good incomes and standards of living, has typically proved problematic, with reintegration hampered by lack of job opportunities.

With its economic focus, this study does not enlarge upon international political sources of domestic conflict, but many examples do of course come to mind in which external political and military factors have played important roles in socio–political stability. During the apartheid era, the front–line states in southern Africa all faced a major external political and military threat, which at times impacted on domestic politics and often provoked internal unrest. Similarly, the Cold War's influence on African domestic politics affected many countries, not least Angola and Mozambique.

The Sources of Disturbance in the Perception of Economic Asset Equilibrium

As noted earlier, a sufficiently substantive revision in *perceptions* of the current distribution of resources, and not necessarily an actual disturbance of it, could suffice to call forth instability. Perceptions may adjust slowly and not reflect any single major factor, but they may also adjust more strikingly after more abrupt changes. Periods of constitutional and electoral reform provide one environment in which changed perceptions may appear and lead to fundamental reappraisals of individuals' and groups' roles in society. This happened in the immediate post–colonial periods throughout Africa. Unfulfilled expectations generated tensions in Zimbabwe. Zambia's programme of Africanisation recognised and sought to address changing perceptions and expectations; while it may have averted a serious black–white confrontation, it may not have averted unrest within the black community.

More recently, changing perceptions appear in states experiencing a move towards a form of democratic rule. For example, it remains to be seen whether post–election expectations in South Africa can be held in check and obvious potential for conflict averted. Such situations raise an important question of causality, with a strong *a priori* case for seeing some simultaneity as changing perceptions stimulate political change. The pre– and post–election periods provide a specific example in which the atmosphere of political debate stimulates a reappraisal of prevailing equilibria; when combined with constitutional reform, the electoral process can provide a major impetus to such a process.

The advent of a peace settlement after protracted civil or international war necessarily raises expectations, not merely of sustained security and a return to normal civilian life, but also of enhanced living standards. In such transitions, rising expectations necessarily encompass reassessment of the relative social standing of individuals and groups, and provide the underlying framework within which new claims and interests will emerge.

The Non–Economic Sources of Instability

While the economic sources of instability hold the primary interest here, one should assess their relative importance *vis–à–vis* non–economic determinants that often have dominated situations of instability. This broader context includes, first, the opportunities for political expression — both the formal political structures and constitutional characteristics of the state, and more *ad hoc* rights and freedoms of expression, such as through the media — and, importantly, how minority groups are managed within political structures. Second, it involves the manner in which human rights are maintained: their legal and constitutional status, together with structures and institutions for implementing the law. Also relevant are the manner of law enforcement, and the independence and integrity of the judiciary, police and armed forces.

Third, it embraces both ethnically based discrimination and other forms of discrimination against identifiable social groups. The role of ethnic questions as determinants of instability and subsequent conflict, and particularly the value of defining conflict as ethnic, has been the subject of intense debate in the literature[17]. Especially since the end of the Cold War at the end of the 1980s, a striking upsurge in intra–state conflict and a parallel decline in inter–state war have occurred, reflecting growing pressures from groups that wish to assert their national identities over those of the state structures[18]. This context makes apparent a closer identification of instability and conflict with disputes between ethnic groupings.

The usefulness of the ethnic label has severe limitations, however. Any economic, social or political problem within a state will inevitably affect groups within the society differently, and thus have a distributional repercussion. The fundamental determinant may well be economic or political, not ethnic *per se*. The central issue involves whether one can relatively easily identify the impact on the basis of clearly definable, ethnically distinct social groupings. If so, an interpretation of ethnic discrimination, intentional or inadvertent, may be appropriate, with a diagnosis of ethnically based instability. Nonetheless, the event provoking the differential distributional effect remains the fundamental determinant.

Relatively liberal use of the term "ethnic" to describe instability is not difficult to appreciate; political leaders of ethnic groups will often see it as of great value in enhancing support from their natural constituencies[19]. Internal rivalry between political leaders will intensify this tendency. Moreover, once an event has stimulated very distinct repercussions on a specific ethnic grouping, with tensions polarised in ethnic terms, a powerful tendency will arise for the same polarisation of other areas of apparent discrimination, thereby further embedding ethnic interpretations in the culture.

In practice, the social structure of most economies will tend to encourage the interpretation of disequilibrating events from an ethnic perspective, because their impact will typically be identifiable to distinct groups. Ethnic groups tend to concentrate in discrete fields of economic activity and perhaps also specific geographical regions[20]. Because a disturbing event will rarely have a uniform, comprehensive impact across society, with a much greater likelihood of focusing predominantly on one or more economic sectors or regions, it becomes easy to interpret events from the ethnic perspective. How much so will depend in part on the history of ethnic relations and the extent of prevailing ethnic sensitivities.

The Emergence of Conflict

The basic causes of a specific outbreak of conflict may not be identical with the proximate ones. Typically, the accumulated stock of outstanding claims by a dissenting group ultimately stimulates one or another form of instability. While a specific event, such as the announcement or implementation of a new government policy, may trigger the onset of destabilising behaviour, the response may more accurately reflect the accumulated set of claims. This explains why the response may *prima facie* appear disproportionate to the apparent issue in question. A more sophisticated variant of this basic argument would add future expectations to the accumulated claims and unfulfilled past expectations that lead to instability. If a group acts with foresight of an emerging policy, even one in only its early stages, the action may again appear disproportionate if one overlooks its longer–term perspective.

A prerequisite for the emergence of instability is the ability of individuals with a common cause to find mechanisms for cohesive expression of their dissent. Individual dissatisfaction, however large the number of individuals, will potentially stimulate instability only if a definable group can mobilise effectively. For example, eliminating consumer–price subsidies in an economic adjustment programme may, *ceteris paribus*, strike heavily on the poorest groups in society, but they typically are too weak politically and too poorly organised to offer a serious threat to social stability. On the other hand, programmes to reduce student grants, as after the devaluation of the CFA franc, focus on groups that are both clearly definable and, perhaps more important, highly organised and capable of expressing forceful dissent.

For all these reasons, the expression of dissent in relatively minor forms of conflict usually begins in urban districts and in structured and organised groupings. As the conflict grows more serious, less coherent urban groupings likely will get drawn into active support for one or another of the opposing factions. In civil wars, the rural population may come to play a critical role as well.

The transition from minor to major instability is perhaps the most important element to analyse — the step from non–violent to violent forms of dissent or, equivalently in many societies, from legal to illegal ones. The former may ultimately hurt economic development as much as the latter, but it is unlikely to erode the economic environment as rapidly and in this sense remains tolerable for longer. While the transition clearly is critical, it is not immediately apparent why it occurs relatively easily in some countries but with far greater reluctance, if ever, in others[21]. The rather naive conclusion that cultural differences prevail adds little to the understanding, although the history of inter–group relationships within a country undoubtedly has fundamental importance. Certainly, in countries that have experienced disturbances and instability over many decades and even centuries, with frequent instances of major instability, a repetition of such events would appear more probable. In others, with traditions of social peace where groups have no history of illegal activities, the step to violence would probably be perceived as one of far more serious import and not contemplated with the same readiness.

The Response to Socio–Political Dissent and Emerging Instability

Why do instability and conflict emerge in some African economies but not in others, despite the apparent presence of many similar problems? This question no doubt reflects an inadequate understanding of the specific determinants of conflict in the economies concerned; apparent similarities often mask more fundamental and critical differences.

The onset of instability and conflict will typically follow a period of social and political tension, in which various social groups signal their dissent and rejection of one or more elements of the economic disequilibrium. The official response during this period will display enormous variation across countries and depend most critically on the nature of the ruling government and its political legitimacy. *A priori*, one would expect that legitimacy derived from military dominance rather than any democratic or quasi–democratic process would permit governments to consider a broader range of responses without fear of electoral consequences. The constitutional basis of the government will also play a major role in the assessment of the validity of the claims of the dissenters. Irrespective of the form of government, this validity will be a central consideration, but autocracies, unlike electorally sensitive governments, will feel greater capacity to implement their subjective political assessments. In general, governments have the option to choose from four generic types of strategies:

a)   *The Pay–for–Peace Strategy*: the government meets the claim of the dissenters, perhaps reversing a recently implemented policy measure or agreeing not to pursue an announced policy decision;

b)   *Alternative Policy Instruments*: the government accedes to the claim, but considers its policy objectives sufficiently critical to merit adopting alternative instruments that serve the same end without provoking the same tensions;

c)   *The Compensating Policy Strategy*: the government does not meet the claim but initiates other measures to compensate the dissenters sufficiently to forestall further instability; and

d)   *The Rejection Strategy*: the government rejects the claim and continues as before, managing dissent and the threat of violence through one of two mechanisms: no action, if it considers the dissent short–lived or likely to wither without serious implications, or repression.

To the extent that governments anticipate accurately the potential for instability, the final strategy appears most likely in view of the political cost of policy reversals, especially with very short lags and in highly visible situations. On the other hand, if they underestimate the potential or do not foresee it, the political and economic cost of one of the first three strategies may do the least damage. These scenarios lead to interesting analysis of the relationship between governments and opposing groups, as in the literature on predation–repression models (see, for instance, Azam, 1995).

In each instance, a government will find itself compelled to consider the net cost of each strategy from the perspectives of political and economic costs. The political cost will depend on factors like the degree of government accountability and a subjective assessment of the likely extent of consensus among the population as a whole regarding the validity of the claim and the implementation of repressive measures. The net economic cost will depend on factors such as whether alternative policy instruments can achieve the same economic objectives, the importance of those objectives and the costs of policy reversal or amendment.

Concluding Remarks

This chapter has sought to set out a framework for the analysis of socio–political instability and for policy thinking. Such a framework must be broad, to capture the immense diversity of conflict situations. The analysis of any specific country will inevitably raise an array of particular considerations, but a framework like this will facilitate their identification and discussion. The treatment here has focused on economic policy, not because this is the only or the pre–eminent issue, but because economic determinants and solutions in conflict situations have received less attention and emphasis than political, diplomatic or military ones. To give thinking in this area a long–term dimension that has often been inadequately addressed, the chapter has also emphasised the fundamental, underlying causes of tension and instability rather than superficial or immediate ones.

Annex

The Analysis of Public Expenditures

The analysis of public expenditures is a key element in the broader analysis of distribution policy and its role in conflict situations, where the allocation of public spending can act as either a causal factor or a potential solution. The degree to which expenditures are thought discriminatory is central, especially from the point of view of dissenting groups. Defining "discriminatory" is difficult in practice, however. Indicators such as expenditures per capita or per region are inappropriate, given that both depend on factors such as the peripherality of different regions, population densities and the geography and terrain. A definition must also address the fundamental question of the objectives of government and its political legitimacy. One objective could be the provision of a single level and quality of service for the population as a whole, with no expectation of equal per capita expenditures across a diverse territory in which the basic conditions of service provision differ markedly. This objective implies, more fundamentally, the inadequacy of considering only the current allocation of both recurrent and investment spending. While it clearly will be important, the *stock* of government assets will have equal and probably more relevance in the near term. Seen from this perspective, a seemingly favourable distribution of current spending may be perceived (rightly or wrongly) as adversely discriminatory given the accumulated stock of service–providing government assets. The converse is, of course, equally possible.

While the prevailing stock of assets undoubtedly acts as a source of instability in many countries, it would be wrong to conclude that, even when broadly accepted as discriminatory, it necessarily results from a long–standing, active policy against one region or group. Situations can exist in which historical expenditure patterns resulted from factors then generally regarded as appropriate, but these underlying factors have undergone changes which now call the previous basis into question. For example, in economies with either nomadic or highly mobile groups, services rarely get provided on a basis comparable to that for services to static, especially urban populations. For education and health services, establishing immobile capital projects for highly mobile populations has limited value. If, however, fundamental group behavioural changes occur, in trends to more sedentary living for example, both group claims and their legitimacy may change markedly. Situations that historically have been acceptable may thus evolve apparently discriminatory characteristics. While government has a clear responsibility to address such emerging needs, one cannot conclude that the new situation results primarily from government policy. Indeed, some groups have seen the provision of some government services as undermining traditional lifestyles and social structures, and have resisted them for that very reason.

Constraints that instability may itself have imposed on expenditure programmes further complicate their analysis. In on–going conflict, trends in expenditures may not reflect the objectives of government, but rather the impracticability of undertaking capital projects, maintenance, or indeed continuing services. Administrators and service providers typically must leave regions in conflict, retreating to the principal urban centres or other regions of the country. Such disruption has often led to severe declines in expenditures and a *prima facie* increase in discrimination, as at times during the conflicts in Angola, Mali and Mozambique, for example. While one should more properly interpret such trends as results rather than causes of instability, they do not necessarily preclude that similar trends prior to the onset of instability were instrumental or causal in provoking it. Understanding the motivations of government adds yet more to the analytic difficulty. The constraint which conflict imposes on expenditure programmes is often legitimate, but many have alleged the use of fiscal programmes as instruments to suppress instability, as a political element in programmes of suppression, and one not required by the exigencies of the conflict itself. The allocation of humanitarian aid provides perhaps the clearest example of the manipulation of expenditures for the political ends of a ruling regime in suppressing instability, but such considerations apply equally to the full range of expenditures.

The foregoing presumes that governments do in fact have control over their expenditure programmes and do prioritise resource allocation according to fixed objectives. In practice, this is a gross exaggeration for many African economies, where a considerable range of decision making lies effectively outside government control whenever expenditure programmes depend heavily on the external donor community for financing. One can argue that governments are always free in principle to reject assistance that does not accord with their development strategies and internal economic constraints, but this is somewhat naive; in practice, they face intense pressure to accept assistance, and their bargaining power in negotiations with donors is relatively weak. Botswana offers an unusual and interesting exception. Elsewhere, many expenditure programmes not only are financially driven by the donor community but are oriented towards programmes it favours. This has familiar implications for the consistency of expenditure programmes with strategic objectives and for the compatibility of recurrent and capital expenditures. The distributional implications are typically less well analysed but, clearly, outlays may not reflect carefully developed distributional policies and have the potential to destabilise.

If a government has objectives that would favour disadvantaged regions or groups, it may face further constraints broadly outside its control, in situations where programmes become blocked or curtailed by a lack of prerequisite resources. One striking example appears in the inability to provide educational and health services in regions of conflict when the appropriate skilled labour has fled or been killed and no financial incentives suffice to attract replacements. This typically occurs in war situations and is an insurmountable obstacle. Another example, not conflict–related but still capable of provoking instability, would involve the absence of a necessary resource such as water[22].

Thus, numerous factors render the interpretation of public expenditure programmes and their historical trends highly problematic. Certainly, the definition and determination of discrimination in expenditure programmes, and an assessment of such factors as important sources of instability, require an intimate understanding of the social and political context in which any expenditure policy has developed.

Notes

1. GDP per capita in Africa fell by 0.76 per cent per annum on average over 1980–92, and before that by an annual average of 0.07 per cent over the 1972–82 period. Thus, while GDP per capita in Africa stood at 33.05 per cent of GDP per capita for the world as a whole in 1972, this share had fallen to 31.04 per cent by 1980, and, more strikingly, to only 24.96 per cent in 1992 (Maddison, 1995).

2. There are many references that set out these fundamental objectives in considerable detail: for example, World Bank (1989).

3. In one sense, these are not secure assets in that the future income is not guaranteed were the government to relocate them. In practice, however, such assets are relatively immobile and the reallocation of the resources is typically only possible at the margin in the short to medium term.

4. Alesina and Perotti (1994) provide a useful review of the methods used by researchers to define and measure instability.

5. The origin and inter–relationship between the traditional, or customary, law and the colonial law is discussed in Mamdani (1995).

6. For a valuable review of the research in this area, see Alberto *et al.* (1994).

7. On the negative impact on investment, see Ben–Habib and Spiegel (1992) and Barro (1991). On the negative impact on growth, see Easterly and Rebelo (1993). Alesina *et al.* (1992) also found that a high propensity to executive change reduced economic growth.

8. As, for example, in World Bank (1989) and Kanbur (1995).

9. Many papers set out the perceived shortcomings of the multilateral institutions' position. For the African perspective, see, for instance, Mkandawire (1995*b*) and M'Baya (1995). Other critiques are put forward in Campbell and Loxley (1989), Beckman (1991) and Gibbons (1994).

10.   This approach should not be confused with those programmes often labelled macroeconomic populism (see Dornbusch and Edwards, 1990), in which there is a concern for growth and distribution that accords too little importance and centrality to the macroeoconomic stability of the economy and the reaction of the international community to the government's programme. Such approaches typically are a response to domestic political pressures to produce rapid results and they generally lead to financial crises that necessitate a policy reversal. Here, the essential concern is the balance of the programme: there is no suggestion that the macroeconomic programme could be given a secondary status.

11.   The withdrawal or curtailment of new food subsidy programmes has been effected in some economies during drought and famine, and has arguably benefited from this apparent external factor.

12.   Ahluwalia and Chenery (1974) make reference to these aspects.

13.   In the African context, see, for example, Mkandawire (1995a). Equally, from their review of the fiscal and political instability channels through which income inequality impacts on growth, Alesina and Perotti (1994) conclude that inequality is an obstacle to growth. A further survey of this literature is provided in Adelman and Robinson (1988).

14.   This categorisation expands that proposed by Ahluwalia and Chenery (1974) in distinguishing the basic approaches to the problem of raising the welfare of low–income groups.

15.   Alternatively, in order to abstract from the problem of an unbalanced budget and deficit financing, regional preference could be measured in terms of the regional imbalance in per capita expenditures. This issue is considered further below.

16.   This analysis does not regard as truly "exogenous" the claims of groups of nationals in voluntary or forced exile, because the fundamental issues in such dissent are more properly seen as internal. Domestic governments have control over these issues, and one can certainly argue that they have a responsibility to diffuse these sources of potential instability before it actually emerges.

17.   For example, in CODESRIA (1993), or in Nnoli (1995) and Mafeje (1995).

18.   These trends are extensively documented in SIPRI (1994), and in other conflict analyses.

19.   This aspect is widely considered in the literature, including, for example, Parenti (1967), Mafeje (1995) and Nnoli (1995). All stress the importance of ethnicity in the domestic political arena in the struggle for power.

20. There are many examples. Geographical differentiation is common. In Nigeria the *Hausa* dominate the north, the *Yorubas* the west and the *Ibos* the east. In Mali the *Tuareg* populate the north and the other major groupings live in the south. Sectoral distribution is also common, ranging from the situation of many east African economies where the Indian or Asian communities dominate many areas of the distribution network, to economies such as Rwanda where the *Tutsi* historically controlled the cattle–owning sector (the major form of disposable wealth), while the *Hutus* traditionally were cultivators in highly populated areas characterised by land shortages and rural poverty.

21. These issues are taken up in Bardhan (1996).

22. This discussion has abstracted from several more mundane issues critical in practical analysis. First, the comprehensiveness of government budgetary data is important, because significant extra–budgetary expenditures will grossly distort assessment of the distribution pattern. Second, analysis faces the difficulty of assessing the relative quality of expenditures, even when the values are available. Third, sheer data availability is a major problem in many economies, particularly for analysis of expenditures below the aggregate economy level. Data for distributional analysis are likely to be far from perfect. Finally, while some studies have looked at the distributional implications of specific projects or programmes where the data have been available, they have largely been confined to analysing the implications for the poorest groups in society, to assess the need for programmes to alleviate the social costs of adjustment processes, and have rarely looked at other issues of distribution, such as allocation among groups, so important to the present context.

Chapter 2

Post–Independence Instability in Mozambique

Introduction

A particularly violent struggle between the FRELIMO Government and the armed opposition forces of RENAMO dominated the post–Independence era in Mozambique. Except for a short period after Independence and a brief lull in the early 1980s, violence very severely disrupted the social and economic life of the entire country until the signing of the Peace Agreement in September 1992. With the extension of RENAMO activity into most rural areas — albeit on an irregular and unpredictable basis — the economy rapidly evolved into isolated urban islands surrounded by a highly insecure countryside. The ultimate restriction of land transportation to a few major routes, and only under military escort, bore striking testimony to the seriousness of the conflict and the degree of economic dislocation achieved by the armed opposition.

The RENAMO forces' classic hit–and–run, guerrilla tactics, rather than clearly established regional zones of control and front lines, characterised the conflict. While areas became recognised as RENAMO strongholds and periodically the focus of Government action, the conflict generally remained unsystematic and geographically widespread. Economic targets, typically the major concern of RENAMO, suffered great destruction with immense accumulated capital losses, including the transportation, power and communications networks and the social services infrastructure.

The extreme violence of frequent atrocities and deep fears of local conflict caused massive human displacements over the entire period. Some 11 per cent of a population estimated at 15 million people in 1975 had escaped internally by the end of the 1980s, fleeing to the relative safety of the outskirts of provincial capitals or district centres; a further 7 per cent fled to neighbouring countries, primarily Malawi, Zimbabwe and Swaziland. Displacement led to ever–increasing reliance on the humanitarian assistance

41

of the external community to sustain the populations. The insecurity affected an estimated further 20 per cent of the population, bringing those seriously touched by the conflict to nearly 40 per cent.

Rural economic activity declined drastically, with both productive and distributive activities effectively wiped out in some areas during the more intense periods of insecurity. Subsistence agriculture became impossible in many regions, and marketed production of both domestic food crops and exports declined dramatically. Heavily oriented towards agro–industrial activities, industry necessarily suffered severely. Mozambique's fundamentally agricultural pre–Independence macroeconomy became grossly destabilised.

The instability had three quite distinct phases.

a)   The pre–Independence conflict lasted from September 1964 until the Lusaka settlement of 7 September 1974, as FRELIMO strove to overthrow the colonial power and establish its own Government.

b)   With the establishment of the FRELIMO Government, Mozambique permitted the Zimbabwe People's Army (ZIPA) to operate from bases within Mozambican territory. With the escalation of the Rhodesian war in 1976, the Mozambican army itself became frequently involved in it, although its exact role is unclear. Also in 1976, Southern Rhodesia established RENAMO, in collaboration with former Portuguese settlers who had left Mozambique. While the Rhodesian interest lay more in monitoring the activities of ZIPA, the Portuguese wanted to destabilise Mozambique. From 1976 to the Independence of Zimbabwe, RENAMO conducted guerrilla operations primarily in the provinces of Tete, Manica and Gaza, with some action in the major cities.

c)   RENAMO was forced out of Zimbabwe when that country became independent in April 1980, but by late 1980 it had transferred its operations to the Transvaal in South Africa. A relative lull ensued in the conflict in 1980 and 1981 as RENAMO re–established itself, with South African support largely replacing Rhodesia's; the conflict took on a new momentum from 1982. Its escalation in the mid–1980s had a serious, cumulative impact on all aspects of economic life until the signing of the Peace Agreement in September 1992.

Fundamental Determinants of Instability

An understanding of the determinants of instability in Mozambique requires differentiation between the motivations of those who financed and actively supported the conflict and those of the RENAMO leadership. Considerable controversy surrounded these issues throughout the war. While the supporters' motivations appeared relatively transparent, even if the exact nature of their support often encountered heated debate, RENAMO's motives were less clear. Many observers contested that they shared the views of their sponsors on any consistent basis.

The conflict spanned about 16 years, but the underlying rationale of the war's primary sponsors changed relatively little. It derived from the complex conjuncture of three political elements:

a)   Groups which had opposed FRELIMO's liberation war and still sought to overthrow the new Government. Ex–colonial Portuguese settlers displaced as the Independence struggle came to its conclusion and individuals or groups which had failed to benefit from the regime change as they had anticipated formed the bulk of this opposition;

b)   Groups ideologically opposed to the political stance of the new Government, specifically its avowed Marxist–Leninist ideology, and intent on establishing a politically more acceptable alternative; and

c)   The stance of the new FRELIMO Government towards the white–minority governments of Rhodesia and South Africa, and the policies these governments pursued towards the front–line states.

The first two elements indicated groups that shared the ultimate objective of overthrowing the Government, but the third reflected more complex motivations. South Africa certainly wanted more to destabilise the Government and prohibit Mozambique from developing into a strong base from which South African security could come under threat; it arguably held the country's economic and political weakness as the primary objective rather than the explicit overthrow of its Government.

During the conflict, the FRELIMO Government, with the support of many external observers, argued that RENAMO's objectives remained ambiguous and largely undefined. An analysis of the RENAMO leadership's behaviour supports this view in several respects.

Given its fundamental bases of financial, ideological and military support, RENAMO seemed to represent all the anti–FRELIMO political elements. Broadly, military support largely originated from South Africa, ideological support from anti–Communist groups around the world, and financial help primarily from similar US groups and ex–colonial settlers. All these groups, with distinct but not incompatible motivations, shared similar objectives and therefore felt able to channel their efforts to destabilise the Government through the single body. Yet efforts at intermediation made during the war appeared severely hampered by the weakness of the RENAMO leadership in articulating its political objectives. This further strengthened the view that they were at best indistinct, and more probably extremely ill–defined.

RENAMO conducted its military campaign with little attempt to construct and consolidate a basis of political support amongst the rural population, despite its at least temporary control of large land areas. On the contrary, its treatment of the civilian population, especially women and children, has generally been described as exceptionally aggressive and violent. While often anecdotal, the evidence is compelling, as carefully documented, for example, in the Gersony (1988) study. Drawing on the accounts of substantial numbers of refugees, Gersony concluded that "there were virtually no reports of attempts to win the loyalty — or even the neutrality — of the villagers. The refugees report virtually no effort by RENAMO to explain to the civilians the purpose of the insurgency, its proposed program or its aspirations." Instead, "the relationship between RENAMO and the civilian population... revolves almost exclusively around a harsh extraction of labour and food". Moreover, he found that "the accounts are so strikingly similar by refugees [who had fled from all regions of the country]... that the violence is systematic and co–ordinated and not a series of spontaneous, isolated incidents by undisciplined combatants". While the motivation for the exceptionally violent behaviour of RENAMO — often compared to that of the Khmer Rouge in its barbarity, if not in its scope — remains largely unexplained, the conclusion that RENAMO devoted little if any effort to disseminating a political programme or construct a rural constituency appears firmly grounded.

Even when the Peace Agreement was signed in 1992 and the process towards democratic elections had been put in train, RENAMO initially advocated only a very halting and poorly articulated political programme, despite its historical importance in the conflict and its apparent status amongst a multitude of smaller, emerging political groupings. Thus, RENAMO itself remains something of an enigma, apparently lacking a well–articulated political agenda. Yet it undoubtedly served as the critical instrument for the implementation of the political programmes of the primary opposition forces to FRELIMO, most of which were located outside Mozambique. Moreover, it would be a mistake to assume that the apparent absence or weakness of political incentives within the RENAMO leadership constituted indifference; their armed opposition was both consistent and forceful[1].

Although the subject has remained highly controversial, observers have tried to identify a more coherent set of RENAMO political objectives. Some have asserted that RENAMO sought democratic objectives and a liberal economic system to replace the Marxist–Leninist regime and its highly centralised structure of economic control, but little evidence supports a view that the leadership had this as a coherent policy goal. Others have focused on a more diverse set of issues, including the appeal of RENAMO to Mozambicans of certain ethnic backgrounds, and to those who felt their dominance within the traditional structures of organisation and government threatened. There are claims that RENAMO found considerable support amongst the *Shona*–speaking people of central Mozambique, venting their disaffection with a Government which gave them little representation at the highest levels, and with its hostility towards traditional chiefs, religious leaders and customs. Yet while RENAMO may have been more active in *Shona*–speaking regions and have had leaders from them, little evidence suggests that this ethnic group provided any substantive support. The Gersony study covered *Shona*–speaking people and found no dissension amongst them from the consensus view. Across the country as a whole, even commentators[2] who identify a more positive political programme within RENAMO itself concede a lack of evidence that the population responded positively to any political appeals that RENAMO may have made. At the most, the rural population in some regions may have accorded some passive support to the armed resistance, but this remains only speculation.

One must distinguish between the armed resistance strategy of RENAMO and the political motivation of the leadership itself. Although RENAMO achieved considerable success in implementing its strategy, especially in the comprehensive disruption of economic activity, this does not imply the leadership's commitment to the political agendas of its sponsors, or even to an agenda of its own. Indeed, the consensus is that this probably was not the case and that, while the apparent weakness of the leadership's political motives remains one of the more puzzling aspects of the entire conflict, the principal philosophical and intellectual backing for the conflict came from the external sponsors of the resistance.

The Role of Economic Factors

Several economic pressures impacted on the socio–political climate throughout this period, some generated within the domestic economy and some largely exogenous. It is important to differentiate between those instrumental in heightening instability and those relatively insignificant in the prevailing Mozambique setting.

Endogenous Sources of Instability

Three elements had potential to provide a fundamentally economic motivation for dissent: the economic claims of previous settlers, economic mismanagement in the post–Independence years and the structural adjustment programme of the late 1980s.

The Economic Claims of Previous Settlers. Groups that lost influence and power at Independence had both economic and political grievances. First, they wanted to regain political control of what they deemed their country and restore the previous order, albeit with a different role for the former colonial power. Second, and not unrelatedly, they wished to regain economic assets they had lost. Such were the Portuguese settlers' fears of a FRELIMO Government that between 1974 and 1976 their resident numbers plunged from an estimated 250 000 to 15 000–20 000. Many abandoned their assets, often productive and infrastructural capital in critical economic sectors because white settlers had so thoroughly dominated the economy. The new Government frequently assumed control of them, not so much as an explicit policy of nationalisation[3] or sequestration as to sustain economic activity — although until the Fourth Party Congress of April 1983 official rhetoric was indeed consistent with a dominant economic role for the state. Those who abandoned their assets necessarily suffered economic losses irreversible at least in the short term. The resolution of property rights remains a major legal issue today, highlighted by steps since 1992 to privatise enterprises as a key element of the World Bank–supported structural adjustment programme. Despite external pressures, the identification of property ownership has been both sensitive and difficult.

Economic Mismanagement in the Post–Independence Years. In the early years of Independence, economic policy operated almost exclusively to maintain essential production, services and distribution networks. Colonial rule had effectively segmented the population by race into specific areas of economic activity, with Africans largely confined to subsistence agriculture and a commercial sector dominated by Portuguese settlers and, in distribution, the Asian community. Few Africans had the privilege of operating in these sectors. The departure of most of the Portuguese stripped managers and skilled labour from the urban–based agro–industrial sector, agricultural export crop production, transportation services (particularly the railroads), significant parts of the distribution network and most small urban industrial enterprises. The collapse of production that followed between 1974 and 1977 resulted almost exclusively from this exodus.

The Government moved so fast to take ownership of agricultural and industrial assets largely from pragmatic motives and the fear of total economic collapse. The establishment of state farms throughout the provinces by grouping the more accessible settler farms was widespread. In the north, peasants were urged to establish collective farms on remote abandoned farms to serve as future co–operatives. In distribution, the Government established a panoply of parastatals to assume the previous operations of a multiplicity of private enterprises, to maintain both the domestic and international trading systems as efficiently as possible. These economic measures probably appealed to the philosophical leanings of the new Government and the exodus provided a massive vacuum into which it could move rapidly without opposition or resistance — but little doubt exists that the pace of the programme got driven primarily by the extreme fragility of the systems that remained.

These structural changes had largely been accomplished when the Third FRELIMO Party Congress met in 1977. The Government then provided a more ideological interpretation of economic policy and sought to develop and consolidate its central role in economic management. The Congress set out to emphasise the Marxist–Leninist foundations of the Party in a broadly perceived political shift towards the Soviet model. Further emphasis went to the extension of state production in both agriculture and industry and the role of the parastatals in distribution. State Plans provided formal mechanisms for controlling economic activity, and administered pricing characterised all stages of the production process. Capital–expenditure programmes reflected these orientations. This fundamental approach to economic policy remained intact through 1983.

Considerable evidence suggests that this economic programme failed to establish a sustainable development path and indeed presided over a dramatic collapse of production. Instability surely contributed heavily to the economic failure, and it would be an overstatement to attribute the entire economic collapse to policy. Nonetheless, the Government appreciated the failure and itself initiated a comprehensive reassessment, which began at the Fourth Party Congress in 1983 and subsequently led to a significant redirection of economic policy during 1984 and 1985.

While the foregoing analysis is widely accepted, the question of whether the mismanagement and economic failures of 1976–83 contributed to the instability of the time remains very open. The evidence points to instability created by the emergence of serious armed resistance as causing the economic collapse, and to inappropriate economic policy as exacerbating it. Few indications suggest much reverse causality; economic collapse may have led to serious rural and urban disenchantment with the Government, but it did not provide momentum for substantive expansion of RENAMO's constituency amongst any economic group. While some aspects of FRELIMO's political and economic agenda became extreme, with very aggressive implementation — as in its experimentation with collectivisation and forced labour — little evidence suggests much effect on instability. In the circumstances, RENAMO's brutality and use of coercion and fear on the local population in economic matters must have offered even less attraction than Government policy.

The Structural Adjustment Programme. The Economic Rehabilitation Programme (ERP) began in 1986. Since then, very few incidents have displayed dissent or opposition to the programme itself in a potentially destabilising manner. Peaceful street demonstrations explicitly targeted at specific elements of the programme have showed no potential to evolve into serious instability. Nevertheless, the programme has not been totally accepted and opposition has been forceful. The Government, fearing the threat of RENAMO insurgency, took such intense security measures in all the major urban centres through 1992 that behaviour deemed likely to provoke instability would have encountered little tolerance. Dissenters' anticipation that any serious protest would be rapidly repressed probably sufficed by itself to quell outward signs of opposition. Whether opposition to the ERP would have become violently manifest in the absence of tight security is of course imponderable.

The absence of protests clearly focused against the ERP does not imply that the fundamental conflict remained necessarily unaffected by the form and implementation of the policy. The adjustment programme should have favoured the Government in its conflict with RENAMO; its anticipated benefits largely accrued to rural areas in which RENAMO was more deeply entrenched, chiefly at the cost of the urban populations over which the Government could maintain tight security. Thus, *prima facie*, reform should have encouraged rural support and undermined the RENAMO position. This interpretation, however, is somewhat incomplete.

One major pillar of the adjustment programme clearly focused on the reintegration of the domestic economy with the international economy, primarily through the establishment of a market–determined exchange rate and the elimination of price controls to allow prices to more approximate closely those prevailing on international markets. This would move the internal terms of trade considerably in favour of rural areas producing the prime export products[4], with industries that remained heavily reliant on imported products and urban consumers bearing the most significant costs of adjustment. Yet even prior to the very substantive exchange–rate and official price adjustments implemented from 1986, the parallel market had emerged to play a dominant role; some estimates put parallel–market transactions at around half of aggregate transactions by volume. The parallel exchange rate stood[5] at Mt. 1 600 to the dollar in 1986, compared to the official market rate of Mt. 40. Thus the real economy had already made significant adjustment towards a market–based economy, and the costs of the official adjustment implemented through the ERP were substantially less dramatic than official policy announcements might have implied. In rural areas, despite the official monopoly of the state parastatals in distribution of most crops, parallel markets had become pervasive. Even before official prices moved progressively up towards international levels and many prices became completely free, many rural producers and consumers had already operated under market prices.

Moreover, even if official price adjustments had the potential to enhance incentives to rural producers and significantly to increase their incomes, it remains unclear how comprehensively and effectively the policy adjustments got communicated throughout the economy in the serious security situation. Many other factors also influenced the rural production incentive structure and made the responsiveness of producers to the policy changes appear modest at best. For instance, the immense destruction of the transportation and distribution infrastructure created a physical barrier to product flows to and from rural areas, compounded greatly by the threat of attack. These factors alone sufficiently explain the isolation of rural producers from centrally determined economic policy and that policy's weak impact on both production and, in all probability, the political attitudes of the rural population.

Economic reform, therefore, probably did not affect substantially the overall well–being of rural producers during the conflict itself; at best, the benefits and response were modest[6]. It is equally doubtful that the reforms significantly changed the political leanings of the rural population and thus its attitudes towards the Government and RENAMO in the ongoing conflict. Disenchantment with the Government, if it existed in rural areas, most probably emanated from the Government's failure to provide an acceptable degree of security that would allow economic activity to proceed unhindered by attack, rather than from dissatisfaction with economic policy itself. Once again, considering RENAMO's behaviour, while the Government may not have extracted significant rural political benefits from its economic programme, it is highly improbable that RENAMO attracted any sympathy either.

Three exogenous economic elements either impinged on the distribution of economic and political power within the country or affected important social groupings within society. The first was international financial assistance, the second hinged on South African employment policy through its effects on Mozambique expatriates and the third involved trends in international commodity prices.

The Role of International Financial Assistance. The complexity of Mozambique's foreign relations is best illustrated by the international alliances that it forged in the 1980s. The Soviet bloc (notably the USSR and East Germany) provided major military advice and hardware, both through finance on concessional terms and in return for privileged access to offshore prawn resources. The bloc played the principal military role, although minor assistance came from some western states, notably the United Kingdom in military training. At the same time, the 1980s saw a major expansion of western developmental and humanitarian aid, initially on both concessional and non–concessional terms, but increasingly the former and in substantial quantities.

This wide range of international assistance reflected Mozambique's strategic role in two of the most critical international political issues of the time: first, the reflection of the Cold War in the developing countries and, second, the stability of the white South African Government. The one helps explain Eastern–bloc military assistance and the other western development assistance, but only with some oversimplification; western development assistance, at least in part and from some governments in the donor community, aimed to reduce the FRELIMO Government's dependence on the communist bloc, notwithstanding that the fungibility of finance made this a murky enterprise.

Not in doubt is the rapid growth of external capital flows during the instability and the role that they played in establishing and maintaining the legitimacy and functioning of the Government. The massive growth in flows of financial assistance to the Government throughout the war (Table 2.1) make readily apparent how such finance came to dominate economic policy thinking. Moreover, the anticipation of a decline — both in military aid, as the Cold War came to an end after 1989, and in development assistance, as donors' domestic budgetary problems intensified and a perceived donor fatigue emerged — had a major impact on the conflict itself. Figure 2.1 identifies trends in the levels of debt outstanding and disbursed over the conflict period[7]. The dominance of the former centrally planned economies (CPEs) until 1985 is clearly apparent, whence the start of the ERP brought sharply accelerated multilateral lending and, given the implicit if not explicit cross–conditionality within the donor community, parallel growth in OECD bilateral lending. Shifting influence, notably in economic policy, accompanied the shift in financing patterns. These trends were greatly accentuated after 1989; the significant collapse of the former CPE share in the early 1990s, mirrored by the rapid growth of both OECD bilateral and multilateral aid, became important contributory factors in the eventual peace settlement.

Table 2.1. **Dependence on External Financial Flows, 1980–94**

	1980–81	1983–85	1987–89	1993–94
Aggregate external assistance ($ billion)	0.67	0.76	1.05	1.14
Aggregate external assistance[1]/GDP	0.28	0.28	0.78	0.78
Debt stock (% of GDP)	n.a.	78.5	321.7	368.3
Debt–service ratio[2] (pre–debt relief)	53.6	180	198	127
Grants (as percentage of MLT plus grants)	8.7	32.2	56.4	0.71
Estimated additional emergency aid ($ million)	52.0	121.7	145.0	n.a.

1. Medium– and long–term loans, official grants and debt relief (arrears included).
2. As percentage of exports of goods and services.

Figure 2.1. **Debt Outstanding and Disbursed, 1985–94**

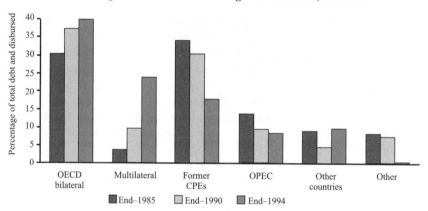

These flows served many of the Government's political objectives. In the face of serious political challenge, international aid necessarily implied its recognition and acceptance as the country's legitimate Government. Internal dissension received little external political support, whether originating in the conflict with RENAMO or from resistance sympathisers who kept their dissent within the legitimate constitutional framework[8]. This point has two caveats. First, RENAMO received major political support from the Government of South Africa, at least for a considerable time, and apparently from Portuguese and American political groups. Second, other governments sometimes displayed political ambiguity. Some supported FRELIMO consistently in its response to South African destabilisation efforts, its anti–apartheid stance and its fight against RENAMO, but had considerable difficulty reconciling themselves to its political and philosophical leanings. While those leanings softened considerably and became widely viewed as replaced by a greater pragmatism that accepted the necessity of economic reforms, the early political and economic policies gave pause to some administrations. For many years, the United States confined itself to humanitarian assistance, with no development aid on any significant scale. The multilateral financial institutions, while formally maintaining their neutrality in political matters, provided substantial development finance from 1986 onwards.

Massive financial inflows undoubtedly prevented total economic collapse. In their absence, and even with the termination of debt service payments, the resources available to finance imports would have plunged, leaving little doubt that both investment and consumption would have collapsed, the latter leading to a major humanitarian disaster. Lost investment finance could perhaps have been tolerated for a time; its impact was in any event overwhelmed by the war's destruction of capital. As the war progressively confined most investment to urban areas, less or no external aid would have accelerated this trend but not had a substantively different impact. In urban areas, lost external aid would have had more devastating effects on living standards, already low at the war's onset and further reduced during it. The provision of consumer goods played a crucial role, either through emergency relief programmes that supported both the displaced and the long–standing urban poor or through augmenting the flow of goods to markets. These goods[9] (especially food imports) substituted for the loss of subsistence agriculture among displaced persons and of a substantial proportion of the rural surplus historically marketed domestically. The potential impact of reduced aid had a real illustration in 1983–85, when aid did drop significantly prior to its rapid growth in 1986 following agreement with the World Bank and IMF on the ERP. Production fell dramatically.

Without the aid flows and the essential products they provided, serious socio–political instability might well have emerged, although this is conjecture. Had famine and deep social distress compounded the impact of the conflict, the stability of the Government would more likely have come under threat. Thus, given the exceptionally precarious existence of many millions of people concentrated around the urban areas, the international community did play a key role in preserving stability and effectively supported the FRELIMO Government in its wider political and military objectives. This conclusion applies with equal vigour to both humanitarian aid and more traditional development assistance.

The large aid flows also implicitly financed the Government's campaign against the RENAMO resistance. Although only the Eastern bloc countries (and the United Kingdom to a much smaller extent) explicitly supported the military programme, the fungibility of inbound funds necessarily permitted internal financing of the war effort with less painful implications for other domestic programmes already under heavy pressure from the fiscal crisis. International donors no doubt fully understood this, but remained content to maintain if not augment their support, provided their own funds went explicitly to non–military uses, a condition the Government fulfilled with little apparent difficulty. Whether or how much concessional external financing impinged on the conflict itself remains a matter for speculation. Militarily, it is impossible to surmise how RENAMO might have responded, and how effectively, to a weakened Government military effort which less external support might have necessitated.

Employment Policy in South Africa. Throughout this period, substantial numbers of Mozambicans found both legal and unofficial employment in South Africa, particularly in mining. This had major microeconomic and macroeconomic implications within Mozambique, with significant numbers of households becoming dependent on the repatriated earnings of relatives in South Africa, and with the remittances making a significant contribution to a fragile balance of payments. The situation suffered from extreme volatility, however, given South Africa's periodic attempts to reduce its dependence on expatriate labour. The numbers of Mozambican miners officially employed in South Africa fell sharply from over 118 000 in 1975 to between 41 000 and 45 000 in 1977–83, then rose to around 60 000 in the mid–1980s.

The *metical* value of remittances varied wildly under the joint influence of exchange–rate movements, the numbers of miners employed and wage rates; local incomes and the external account necessarily felt the impact. For example, when expatriate employment fell to its lowest level of just under 40 000 in 1983, remittances actually peaked, as wage increases offset both the decline in numbers and the depreciation of the rand. They then plummeted by more than 40 per cent through 1985, even as employment rose to over 61 000, because the rand fell by 50 per cent against the dollar. Remittances in 1985 stood at less than 75 per cent of their dollar value of 1980. From this low point, revenues revived to around their previous levels; in 1990–94, average annual remittances were little changed in dollar terms from ten years earlier. Yet with the massive depreciation of the *metical* since 1986, remittances as a proportion of local currency GDP have risen significantly.

Aside from remittance implications, social consequences emerged as the numbers of Mozambican workers benefiting from legal expatriate incomes sank during a time of substantial internal crisis[10]. The numbers of workers in unofficial employment, and of households affected, are of course unrecorded. In general, however, this additional pressure on living standards can only have exacerbated the economic pressures flowing from the conflict itself. Politically, it is doubtful that the Government sustained damage from the repatriation itself, because it reflected a policy decision of the South African Government and more likely reinforced suspicions that the South Africans were set on destabilising the Mozambican economy. Yet the return of the miners, accustomed to relatively good incomes and without much prospect of employment in Mozambique, represented a considerable threat to social stability. In many respects, this foreshadowed the far more serious problem that would arise with the demobilisation of troops after the signing of the Peace Agreement in 1992. In the 1980s, however, social instability carried with it the potential for ebbing support for FRELIMO and tacit, if not active, support for RENAMO.

Trends in International Commodity Prices. One of the principal elements of the ERP was the restoration of producer incentives, particularly price incentives for export crops. Price reforms made consistent and substantive progress after 1986, but price trends in international commodity markets partly undermined this success. Table 2.2 illustrates the decline in real world prices for two key Mozambican export products during the 1980s. The real price of cashew collapsed by 1989 to only 56 per cent of its 1981 level, and that for cotton fell to under 70 per cent. Despite an improvement in the relative price of Mozambican cashew on the world market and a stable relative price for cotton, dollar export prices declined significantly.

Table 2.2. **Trends in International Commodity Prices**
(1981 = 100)

Export Product[1]	1989
Cashew:	
World price ($ constant price)	56.0
World price ($ current price)	73.5
Mozambique export price ($ current price)	84.2
Export: World price ratio (current price)	114.6
Cotton:	
World price ($ constant price)	69.9
World price ($ current price)	91.4
Mozambique export price ($ current price)	91.8
Export: World price ratio (current price)	100.4

1.   Mozambique export prices are fab Mozambique. Dollar prices are per kg.
Source: World Bank (1990*a*).

The chronic disequilibrium of the external account cannot be attributed primarily to these trends because any export price effects were consistently dwarfed during this period by import and export volumes. Adverse trends in the external terms of trade did have significance in countering the incentive benefits that flowed from the policy reforms. They weakened the political standing of a Government under considerable pressure after 1986 to demonstrate the positive benefits from the adjustment process when only the costs were immediately apparent. While it is doubtful that this depressive influence would by itself have been sufficient to perpetuate the war or to push the rural population into explicit or passive support of RENAMO, it represented another contributory factor that weakened the potential political pay–off from adjustment.

The Direct Impact of the Conflict

The identification of the economic impact of the conflict in Mozambique presents many problems. Aside from obvious deficiencies of the data and difficulties in interpreting the numbers, the major determinants of economic development in this period are not readily isolated but had very substantive influence. Five of them were key:

a) *The conflict itself.* It spanned three periods: 1964–73 (the war for independence in Mozambique), 1975–79 (the war for independence in Southern Rhodesia and limited RENAMO activity), and 1980–92 (the main period of RENAMO activity against the FRELIMO Government);

b) *The mass exodus* of Portuguese settlers, notably in 1974–76. Such were its magnitude and the strategic importance of the settlers, established by design under the colonial regime, that the exodus had immense immediate and long–term economic repercussions;

c) *The Peace Agreement,* from September 1992;

d) *The economic and social policy of the Government,* which underwent a major transformation in the mid–1980s. It developed with the change of thinking of Samora Machel from 1980 and, particularly, the Fourth Party Congress of 1983. After these conceptual shifts, more substantive policy changes dated from 1985 and the subsequent involvement of the IMF and World Bank; and

e) *Climatic trauma.* Droughts (1982–85 and 1991–92) and floods (1977–78) had heavy effects on agricultural production and agro–industry.

Table 2.3 attempts a summary of this array of determinants, which often overlapped in timing and impact. The complexity of these overlaps and the difficulty of isolating years in which "other things equal" would reasonably approximate reality make highly debatable any identification of appropriate periods for comparative analysis. Moreover, lags in the economic system often spread the impact of these events over many years.

With the foregoing caveats, two pairs of periods may be tentatively identified for comparisons[11]. First, to address the impact of the conflict in the absence of economic reform, 1979–81 represents a time of relative peace, with RENAMO preoccupied by the end of the Rhodesian war and its relocation to South Africa, and 1983–85 one in which the war escalated severely. Second, to assess the war's consequences during economic reform, 1987–89 saw intense conflict and 1993–95 the dramatic return to stability following the Peace Agreement. RENAMO's policy of explicitly targeting the economic infrastructure brought immense accumulated destruction which had impact on virtually all areas of economic activity. The following sections summarise this impact in terms of the human cost, production levels, and the economic and social infrastructure.

Table 2.3. **The Primary Periods of Development, 1970–95**

Years	Events
to 1973	War of Independence
1974–76	Independence; exodus of colonial settlers
1976–79	Post–Independence; Rhodesian war; limited RENAMO operations
1980–81	Zimbabwe Independence; transfer of RENAMO operations to South Africa
1982–83	Escalation of RENAMO bases
1984–85	Continuing RENAMO operations; preparations for policy reform
1986–91	Continuing RENAMO operations; implementation of policy reforms
1992	Peace Agreement
1993 to present	Continuing policy reform

The Human Cost

The rural civilian population largely bore the human costs of the war, so any attempt to quantify those costs would be highly questionable; little systematic evidence exists, although anecdotal information on specific military operations and specific atrocities is available. The independent study undertaken by Robert Gersony (1988) for the US Department of State represents one of the few attempts to analyse and quantify the conflict's impact. It estimated, conservatively, that around 100 000 civilians had been killed, with many thousands severely injured, abused and mutilated from Independence to the end of 1987.

General rural disruption affected virtually the entire country for much of the time from the early 1980s until the Peace Agreement. The threat or reality of personal attack dominated almost all rural life, with massive population displacement both within the country and to neighbouring states. By mid–1989, an estimated 1 million people (7 per cent of the total population of around 15.2 million) had become refugees in neighbouring states, with a further 1.7 million (11 per cent) displaced within Mozambique. A further 2.9 million (19 per cent) remained subject to constant disruption by the conflict. Most of the internal refugees concentrated around the provincial and district capitals, where they could find relatively good security and food supplied from humanitarian aid.

Economic activity in Mozambique since Independence obviously has suffered from great volatility (Table 2.4). Two periods of severe economic collapse stand out: one coinciding with the exodus of skilled labour in 1974–76, when the economy contracted at almost 10 per cent a year on average, and the other during 1982–85, when aggregate GDP dropped at an average annual rate of almost 6 per cent. The second period is clearly associated with the intensification of the conflict in 1982 and its comprehensive impact on rural areas. It also reflects serious droughts, which hit agricultural production particularly in the southern and central regions. In contrast, Mozambique also has had two periods of relatively good growth: first in the immediate post–Independence years from 1977 through 1981, when GDP growth averaged a little over 2 per cent a year, and then since 1986. Apart from 1992, when serious drought again touched southern Africa, the years after 1986 have seen growth rates reaching around 5 per cent on a more consistent and stable basis.

Table 2.4. **The Impact on Growth**

	Before Economic Reform Programme		During Economic Reform Programme	
	1979–81	1983–85	1987–89	1993–94
	Peace	Conflict	Conflict	Peace
Real GDP	1.00	–6.58	5.46	9.67
Gross social product: aggregate	2.88	–11.82	4.31	11.00
Agriculture	0.47	–6.53	5.71	13.15
Industry	4.66	–19.90	7.77	–5.00
Services	n.a.	–1.53	3.83	18.50

Note: All figures are annual average percentage changes. The real GDP figure for 1993–94 includes the estimated figure for 1995.

Table 2.4 also shows how growth performance bifurcated between the periods before and after economic reform began, with the impact of the conflict overlaid on both. Before reform, when centralised administration of a command economy played the dominant role, the conflict appears to have dramatically enfeebled an already very weak growth path[12]. Even in the relatively good performance of 1979–81 when real GDP was rising at 1 per cent a year, per capita GDP declined by between 1.5 per cent and 2.0 per cent annually. During the second pre–reform phase, growth turned disastrously negative under the combined effects of the resurgence of conflict and the drought; their relative importance resists disentanglement. After reforms began, performance generally improved markedly, notwithstanding the dampening effects of the continuing war in 1987–89. Growth then accelerated significantly after the Peace Agreement, although the 1992 drought hit hard and the rebound from it in 1993 (almost 19 per cent) distorts the average upward. In fact, economic expansion settled at around 5 per cent in both 1994 and 1995, little different as yet from before 1992, when conflict still raged but reform was in full swing.

On balance, these periods probably are too short to support meaningful conclusions, especially regarding post–conflict performance. While the conflict ended in 1992, its economic repercussions linger and still prevail over a wide range of economic activity. The restoration of the economic and social infrastructure will certainly extend over the long term, and the effects of severe infrastructural weaknesses will persist. Similarly, the repatriation of refugees did not commence until 1993 and remains in train; this delays the resumption of both subsistence and market production. Until the constraints imposed by the conflict ease, the economic response to the peace will clearly take considerable time to emerge fully.

Export and disaggregated sectoral data (Figure 2.2 and Table 2.5) reflect the same story. They reveal the comprehensive impact of the conflict. The industrial sectors — largely agro–industrial and heavily dependent on agricultural performance — showed high vulnerability to the disruption of rural production. Exports, dominated by output from the state farms and plantation agriculture, both of which RENAMO targeted throughout the conflict, had even more dramatic declines. Aggregate export volumes plunged by an estimated annual average of around 34 per cent in 1982 and 1983. Tea and sisal production, once major elements of export revenue, almost stopped, while cashew exports fell to around 20 per cent of their 1980 level by 1985. Cotton exports proved relatively resilient to the conflict for many years, but they too collapsed by the mid–1980s. Since the ERP began, the performance of some exports (cashew especially) has been highly volatile and, in some instances, difficult to explain from the perspective of either economic reform or conflict.

Figure 2.2. **Export Volumes, 1973-94**

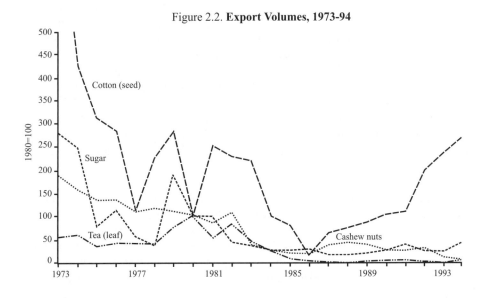

57

Table 2.5. **The Impact on Export Growth**
Sectoral Impact

	Before Economic Reform Programme		During Economic Reform Programme	
	1979–81 Peace	1983–85 Conflict	1987–89 Conflict	1993–94 Peace
Cotton (seed)	3.8	–30.0	83.9	16.4
Tea (leaf)	5.9	–58.4	–60.6	41.4
Sugar	36.8	–16.0	–12.8	27.1
Cashew nut	–10.2	–42.7	24.7	–59.6
Total Exports	–2.2	–33.9	9.3	2.7

Note: Export volumes (annual average percentage growth). Implicit volumes derived from value and price data.

To sum up, the Mozambique conflict had a devastating effect on all elements of economic life. The inability to confine it geographically brought the disruption of most rural production and, given the high degree of sectoral interdependence, of urban production as well. Moreover, the disruption was neither consistent nor uniform, so the threat of insecurity created sufficient uncertainty effectively to eliminate activity in extensive areas of the country. The collapse of the real economy became inevitable, which would also have been the fate of the financial accounts but for external assistance on a massive scale.

Impact on Economic and Social Infrastructure

Energy. The conflict severely disrupted energy transmission and distribution, which fed back to deep cuts in production. Hydroelectric generation collapsed, from 10 700 gigawatt hours (gWh) in 1980 to 5 700 gWh in 1983 and only 173 gWh in 1986. The electricity transmission grid was almost completely destroyed by 1983, and power exports (9 500 gWh in 1980) virtually ceased from 1984 onwards. RENAMO cut the rail link between Moatize and Beira in 1983, which severely constrained coal transport and effectively ended both domestic and international coal shipments (Table 2.6 shows the effects on coal output and exports). Thus, the war rendered almost non–operational Mozambique's two major energy production sources, the Cahora Bassa hydropower station and the Moatize coalfield. By 1986 the economy had been deprived of an estimated $8.4 million annually from lost electricity exports and another $4 million from lost coal exports.

Transport. Before the conflict took hold, transport policy had accorded only low priority to maintenance of the infrastructure. The war both compounded this problem and added massive physical destruction. By the late 1980s, over 70 per cent of the tertiary road network (gravel) was deemed in poor condition — plus an estimated 60 per cent of the secondary network (also gravel), as against only 20 per cent in 1973. As Table 2.7 shows, road and rail traffic as well as transport revenues fell heavily in the 1980s.

Table 2.6. **The Impact on Coal Production and Exports**
Thousand metric tons

	Before Economic Reform Programme		During Economic Reform Programme	
	1979–81 Peace	1983–85 Conflict	1987–89 Conflict	1993–94 Peace
Coal output (coking and burning)	143.05	25.83	54.75	n.a.
Coal exports	170.05	14.17	15.09	5.03

Note: 1994 data are estimates.

Table 2.7. **The Impact on Transportation**
Freight carried

	Before Economic Reform Programme		During Economic Reform Programme	
	1979–81 Peace	1983–85 Conflict	1987–89 Conflict	1993–94 Peace
Road (million ton/kms)	55.15	34.33	27.10	45.80
Rail total (million ton/kms)	1 373.50	531.00	336.00	651.50
Rail (international) (million ton/kms)	912.70	402.80	160.20	490.50
Transportation revenues ($ million)	87.30	46.77	39.90	72.65

Note: 1994 data are estimates.

Education. Government data record the destruction of over 3 200 primary schools from 1981 to early 1989, more than half of the 1981 stock. Because secondary education tended to be more urban based, it lost around 15 per cent of its schools in 1981. All school losses concentrated heavily in the rural areas. Primary schools lost almost a third of their teaching staff in 1981–87. While some refugee children in neighbouring countries or in the camps surrounding major population centres received some rudimentary education during this time, immense disruption of their education clearly occurred.

Health. In the five years or so through 1980, the new Government had worked hard to increase the number of primary health–care units; posts rose from 326 to 1 191 and health centres from 120 to 251. The conflict wreaked great damage on this infrastructure, with an estimated 196 units (posts or centres) destroyed and another 288 heavily damaged and forced to close by 1985. This amounted to about 34 per cent of the health network. By 1989, an additional 78 units had been destroyed and a further 550 closed.

Medium–Term Impacts

Saving and Investment

Two major problems plague this analysis. The first lies in substantial data inadequacies, notably the absence of national–accounts estimates before 1980 and the general weakness of data compilation throughout the ensuing decade[13]. Second, external assistance dominated investment and saving performance. Aggregate investment data provide little if any indication of investment behaviour in the domestic economy, other than that financed from external savings. This constrains any analysis of the conflict's impact on the domestic potential for medium–term growth to a focus on saving behaviour, although the dominance of external savings makes interpretation difficult here as well[14].

Aggregate investment as a proportion of GDP has gone through three distinct phases since 1980 (Figure 2.3):

a)   1980–82: investment held relatively stable, at around 20 per cent of GDP;

b)   1983–85: investment fell heavily in 1983 and averaged less than 10 per cent of GDP over the period, dropping to 7 per cent in 1985; and

c)   1986–93: investment rose steeply in both local and foreign–currency terms. Its share of GDP jumped from under 10 per cent in 1986 to 33 per cent in 1988 and then to 60 per cent in 1993–94.

Figure 2.3. **Investment and External Capital Inflows, 1980–94**

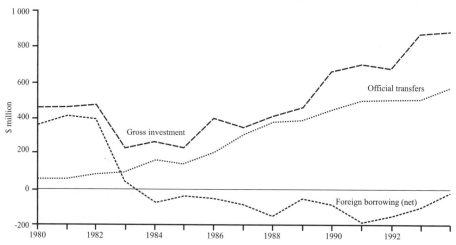

The first period, one of low–level conflict which affected economic activity to only a minor degree and in a confined geographical area, provides a base from which to assess the effects of later escalation of the fighting. Although investment ratios held relatively high, this was not a time of buoyant private–sector confidence and self–sustaining growth. Domestic saving financed investment to only a marginal extent and external savings filled the gap. Gross national saving (GNS) totalled only 3 per cent of GDP, with private–sector saving on average negative at –0.6 per cent and public–sector saving at an average of only about 3.5 per cent. By contrast, external savings excluding official transfers averaged over 16 per cent of GDP, and including them over 19 per cent. While one might view this as a display of some confidence in growth prospects on the part of international investors, most of the external funds came from aid loans and some overly optimistic commercial banks. Foreign direct investment (FDI) probably was minimal; no formal data on it exist.

As the conflict escalated in 1983, the crash in economic activity impacted on saving and investment in important ways. The collapse of production highlighted the extreme fragility of both the real economy and the monetary economy, especially the external account, which saw the debt–service ratio jump to 130 in 1983. External borrowing practically imploded, shifting from an average annual inflow of almost $400 million (1980–82) to a net outflow of over $20 million a year in 1983–85, while unrequited official transfers remained at under 4 per cent of GDP. The apparent stability of external savings in fact reflected a marked build–up of arrears (see Tables 2.8 and 2.9).

Table 2.8. **The Impact on Savings and Investment**

	Before Economic Reform Programme		During Economic Reform Programme	
	1980–81	1983–85	1987–89	1993–94
	Peace	Conflict	Conflict	Peace
Private–sector GNS	-0.60	0.76	-9.61	13.55
Public–sector GNS	3.63	-4.73	14.58	25.07
Aggregate GNS	3.03	-3.98	4.98	38.61
External saving (including transfers)	16.53	13.08	25.88	21.35
External saving (excluding transfers)	18.95	17.95	52.83	57.74
Aggregate investment	19.56	9.13	30.85	59.96

Note: All figures are annual average percentages of GDP.

Table 2.9. **The Impact on Capital Flows**

| | Before Economic Reform Programme | | During Economic Reform Programme | |
| | 1980–81 | 1983–85 | 1987–89 | 1993–94 |
	Peace	Conflict	Conflict	Peace
Foreign borrowing (net)	386.6	-23.3	-99.6	-64.6
Official external transfers	56.7	132.0	356.2	533.9
Gross investment	458.9	242.9	408.1	879.8

Note: All figures are annual average in $ million.

As production and fiscal revenues plummeted, positive but low public–sector saving gave way to dissaving of almost 5 per cent of GDP in 1983–85 (Table 2.8). Meanwhile, private–sector saving apparently turned mildly positive, possibly reflecting the sheer unavailability of consumer goods as distribution systems fell apart. This compensated only very slightly for the loss of external borrowing, however, and investment got relief from a yet more dramatic collapse only through the rapid rise of external debt arrears. Neither domestic saving nor voluntary external saving held it up.

Figure 2.4. **Savings, 1980–94**

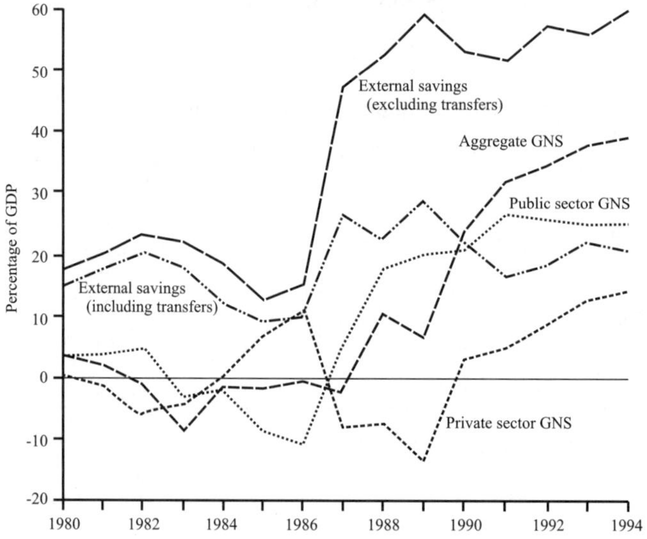

The coincidence of the conflict with the implosion of foreign borrowing obscures more complex causality. The overextension of debt in the early years of the new Government relative to Mozambique's repayment capacity might well have given cause for concern by 1983 and a subsequent curtailment of credit, even absent the effects of war. Past policy mistakes had much to do with the reductions in lending, although the conflict certainly exposed the problem more starkly as it cut capacity to service prevailing debt.

The third phase (1986–93) resembles the first (1980–82), in that investment rose sharply as a proportion of GDP and external savings primarily financed it. It also differs, however, because grant finance replaced commercial and non–concessionary loans in the mix of funds from abroad (Table 2.1). This shift resulted largely from political changes and the institution of extensive policy reform. The period witnessed a move towards heavy fiscal restraint and strongly positive public–sector saving, which averaged over 25 per cent of GDP in 1993–94 (Figure 2.4). Private–sector dissaving initially deteriorated to almost 10 per cent of GDP in 1987–89, then rebounded to net saving of almost 14 per cent of GDP in 1993–94. Thus, GNS improved mightily.

Investment behaviour diverged widely between the private and public sectors in this third phase (Figure 2.5)[15]. Despite the continuing conflict in the late 1980s and early 1990s, private investment responded to the implementation of economic reforms and the steady establishment of a market–based environment. After investing to a markedly lesser extent than the public sector for many years, the private sector became the source of most investment growth after 1988 and its capital outlays relative to GDP exceeded those of Government after about 1991. Definitional problems (see endnote 15) may reduce the precision of this general description, however. Moreover, some external donors strongly directed their aid to private enterprises without necessarily imposing commercial terms, which would have made much private investment supply–driven rather than demand–driven. Incentives to invest generally remained extremely weak.

Figure 2.5. **Investment by Sector, 1980–94**

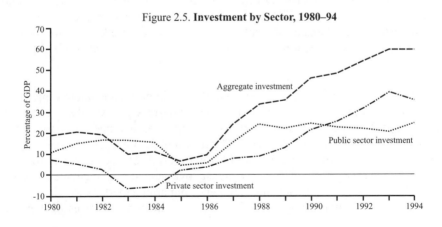

63

In the absence of both incentives and capacity of the domestic private sector to invest, external saving became the central determinant of the long–term development prospects of the economy. The escalation of the war clearly changed the composition of external savings, from non–concessionary to concessionary and from commercial sources to bilateral and multilateral aid, but it clearly did not reduce them. Strong evidence indicates that it increased them, and allowed extremely high investment ratios; the motivations go back to the fundamental political considerations that underlay the conflict.

The war's heavy costs, which paradoxically helped the Government to procure such large and increasing assistance, overwhelmed its superficial benefit, however. The additional external savings compensated only very partially for the conflict's great damage to the development process. Moreover, the changing composition of external savings raised questions about the efficiency with which the resources were deployed. Several studies during the period highlighted the concerns, which focused on the dominant role of donors in allocating investment and the tendency to emphasise large, capital–intensive projects at the expense of maintaining the existing capital stock. High investment levels concentrated on public–sector projects did produce an allocation pattern different from that which would have obtained with a larger private–sector role. Nevertheless, one can argue that the Government had a correct focus as war raged: to maintain as best it could the economic and social infrastructures, support current production and distribution, and sustain a longer–term basis for private investment after the violence ended.

Fiscal Policy

The escalation of the conflict in the early 1980s cut deeply into the tax revenue yield, as production slumped and the administrative structures for tax collection in many regions of the country collapsed. Tax revenue fell from around 15 per cent of GDP in 1980–81 to a low of 9 per cent in 1985–86. With the introduction of major new fiscal measures under the ERP in 1986, the tax take began to recover. The measures aimed to restore fiscal balance and cut official resort to the banking sector to zero as fast as possible. Tax collections jumped back to over 20 per cent of GDP by 1989 (Figure 2.6).

These changes generated concern about their impact on economic incentives. The war had effectively confined tax collection to progressively smaller economically active groups. Between 1986 and 1989, for example, tax revenue as a proportion of *marketed* GDP rose from an estimated 14.4 per cent to 32.3 per cent, far above the tax to aggregate GDP ratio of 20.7 per cent in 1989. Before 1986, the drastic narrowing of the tax base had arisen as much from the grossly overvalued exchange rate as from the conflict, because it had stimulated the emergence of parallel markets which had driven activity out of the formal, tax–paying economy. Exchange–rate reforms weakened but by no means eliminated the parallel markets, and they did expand the tax base somewhat. Yet very high effective tax rates on the taxable economy remained because the war had taken extensive rural areas essentially out of it.

Figure 2.6. **Revenues and Expenditures, 1980–94**

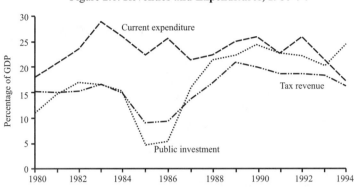

Recurrent outlays rose steadily as a proportion of GDP in 1980–83, then stabilised at around 25 per cent in 1984–92 (Figure 2.6). Although the pressures of war should have pushed them up even more, significant areas of the country became subject to only weak administrative coverage, and the provision of public services fell sharply with the destruction of their infrastructure. The conflict was associated with some resource reallocation, although the available data allow only a fairly aggregate analysis of it. Recurrent outlays on defence moved up only modestly in 1982–83 but rose to some 42 per cent of the total in the second half of the 1980s, then eased to about 34 per cent after the Peace Agreement (Figure 2.7). Doubts plague the reliability of these data, making the description indicative but certainly not definitive. Significant amounts of military (and non–military) expenditure are believed to have been kept off–budget, especially in the first half of the 1980s, and only fragile accounting processes were in place at the time. Central budgeting processes came progressively into effect and off–budget activities were curtailed if not eliminated with the ERP reforms — but necessary military confidentiality and funding from the Eastern bloc kept substantial military outlays from accurate budgeting.

A decline in educational expenditures coincided with the increase in military outlays; they dropped from around 17 per cent of recurrent spending in 1979–81 to about 12 per cent in the late 1980s and early 1990s. It is not clear how much of this drop reflected budgetary pressures and how much was forced by the rural impact of the conflict. Health expenditures dipped in 1983–85 but then recovered, despite the loss of much delivery infrastructure. The Government had accorded high priority to social–service outlays since Independence and it remained reluctant to make major cuts, while the external–donor community played a major role in maintaining these services in the face of severe financial restraint. Indeed, following the introduction of the ERP in 1986, with its tight fiscal stance, cuts in social outlays would have been all the greater had draconian reductions not hit other budget areas, notably subsidies to enterprises and, later, consumer goods.

Figure 2.7. **Recurrent Expenditures, 1980–94**

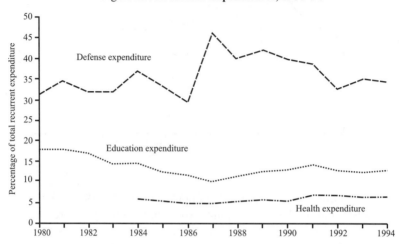

The Restoration of Stability

The history of Mozambique's many years of internal conflict suggests that economic policy played only a modest role in attempting to restore socio–political stability, and that non–economic, indeed often external, factors had overwhelming influence. The years after the Peace Agreement saw a marked change. Economic policy received a key role in the complex processes of disarmament, demobilisation, reintegration and resettlement — a role correctly considered critical for establishing a sustainable peace and averting degeneration into renewed civil conflict and disorder. Lessons from Angola in the early 1990s had revealed very clearly the costs of mishandling transition. Political figures from both within Mozambique and the international community went to considerable pains to minimise risks that the Peace Agreement would collapse, placing a particular emphasis on quartering and disarming RENAMO's and FRELIMO's rival armies and forming a united national army prior to moving ahead with the democratic process, especially multi–party elections.

The General Peace Agreement of 4 October 1992 brought a rapid transformation from insecurity, especially in rural areas, to, indeed, general peace[16]. It envisaged a timetable of actions leading to multi–party elections in October 1993. The two main steps involved ratification of the Agreement by the National Assembly and approval of the mandate and budget for United Nations operations in Mozambique (UNOMOZ) to oversee the demobilisation programme. Commissions were established to implement the Agreement and a new Electoral Law needed preparation. The agreed cease–fire held, but the process moved very slowly in its early stages, raising fears of regression into further conflict. Long–standing political disputes between RENAMO and the Government persisted, stalling progress towards elections; negotiations over the new Electoral Law were not resolved until October 1993. The UN Security Council did not approve the mandate of UNOMOZ until December 1992, and this delayed other action. The departure of foreign troops from Mozambican soil, key to the Agreement, occurred only in June 1993, when the Zimbabwean and Malawi armies finally withdrew from defence of their transport routes to the sea.

Greater concern arose from delay in the critical timetable for quartering and demobilising the opposing forces. Disagreement between their leaderships created the central problem, although all agreed that a sudden resumption of hostilities had a low probability. Equally critical, the UN troops arrived late, ten months after signature of the Agreement, in June 1993. All this led to an October 1993 revision of the timetable for implementation of the Agreement. Demobilisation would now occur between December 1993 and May 1994, with elections put back to October 1994.

Thus, 1994 became the pivotal year. Mozambique's first multi–party elections, judged free and fair by the international community, saw 85 per cent to 90 per cent of the population voting — notwithstanding that the Agreement was only two years old and despite the resettlement between October 1992 and September 1994 of 3.2 million displaced people and 1 million refugees from abroad. That year also brought the demobilisation of 80 000 soldiers and establishment of the new, combined army.

Economic policy aimed to help restore peace in two ways: first, through consolidation and further development of the adjustment and reform programme initiated years before in 1986; and, second, through specific measures targeted towards faster, more sustainable transition. Uppermost was the need to demobilise unneeded troops and resettle them, along with both domestic and foreign *deslocados*. The authorities saw resettlement in traditional homeland areas as crucial both to disperse potentially large groups of ex–soldiers with the power to initiate unrest and to reduce burdens on the cities to which people had gravitated to escape rural danger. It also helped to facilitate rapid reduction of defence expenditures to make room for the vast financial requirements of the reintegration programme[17].

The Government adopted a three–pronged strategy for restoring stability and economic development:

a) *Stronger governance.* This encompassed first the consolidation of democracy, through defining and ensuring the effective operation of multi–party institutions, including the elected Assembly, its structure of parliamentary commissions and press freedoms. Second, it sought stronger legal processes and structures, which entailed better internal security and maintenance of law and order and required addressing questions of financial accountability, corruption and a stronger judicial structure;

b) *Policies to promote economic and social resettlement and restoration of normal rural life*; and

c) *Economic policy for sustainable growth*, with a framework for private–sector development, a scheme to prioritise public investment in economic and social infrastructure rehabilitation (particularly human resource development), and export promotion to restore external financial balance.

This approach had as its fundamental philosophy the idea that economic development, growth and, especially, employment generation, combined with an appropriate distributional emphasis, would secure an environment for sustaining the political peace process. The more rapid the return to economic and social normality in people's lives, the more likely the prospect of balancing and resolving the competing demands of former combatants. Economic stability was thought basic to the restoration of political and social stability. In its absence, further conflict was greatly feared.

The first element in the three–pronged approach focused on establishing an institutional framework with the capacity to accommodate a more pluralistic society and provide competing groups with the necessary channels for expression without recourse to conflict. The second and third aimed for economic development. The approach acknowledged the twin needs of a growth strategy and a distributional programme. The former was essential both because internally generated resources remained extraordinarily low with a severe problem of structural poverty and because external finance was unsustainable, even if it might alleviate short–term crises. The latter had several dimensions: it needed to address competing demands of former RENAMO and Government supporters; it had to satisfy those returning from internal and external exile as well as those who had remained in extreme rural deprivation; and it was constrained because vast numbers of Mozambicans still lived in exceptional poverty only aggravated by the long conflict.

Over 4 million internal and external refugees had returned to their traditional homes by October 1994, but more than another million still needed resettlement. Resettlement programmes to restore people's livelihoods had paramount importance, particularly in the rural areas, making agricultural and rural policies, both immediate and long–term, key to the resettlement effort. They had five key objectives:

a)   provision of potable water;

b)   rehabilitation of the rural economic infrastructure, especially access to roads and markets;

c)   provision of seeds, through either markets or external aid;

d)   a transparent process for land allocation, plus regularised legal rights for existing and new occupants; and

e)   enhanced productivity of cultivated land and reduced post–harvest losses.

To accompany these direct agrarian policies for productivity and a sustained resettlement process, other economic policies aimed explicitly at the economic and social integration of demobilised troops. Their key components included vocational training programmes, promotion of local micro–enterprises and co–operatives for goods and services, securing the aid of NGOs and other institutions to promote integration projects, and stimulation of soldiers to seek financial and other support for their own integration.

The entire approach worked. It both defused potential tensions and re–established a degree of normality in a relatively short time. Yet it was by no means sufficient. It needed tangible international support, which came slowly at first.

This chapter has highlighted that external factors predominated over internal or ethnic considerations as causal in Mozambique's post–Independence conflict. One might expect the removal of many of them to have made the transition to peace less fragile, in contrast to many other national conflict situations where basic internal sources of conflict may be left unresolved by a peace accord. Yet, while the exhaustion from 20 years of war together with much weaker internal forces for conflict made a resumption of major hostilities unlikely, other dangers remained real. Chief among them was the spectre of sliding into a disintegrated and chaotic economy with little political administration to hold the country together. The post–Agreement economic programme played a key role in establishing normal rural and urban economic life and in restoring growth as well as socio–political cohesion and stability.

Notes

1. For much of the period of conflict, it was widely assumed that the RENAMO leadership's control over its organisation was weak, and that a peace settlement would encounter a major problem of enforcement, or at best a significant lag in its effective implementation. In the event, however, RENAMO showed considerable control, suggesting that it may have been better co–ordinated throughout the period than many thought.

2. As, for example, in Nelson (1984).

3. Such enterprises became termed "intervened" enterprises in acknowledgement that the state had not formally nationalised the assets, but had acquired them typically after abandonment.

4. It is reasonable to assume that, throughout this period, Mozambique was a price taker on international markets.

5. The currency is called the metical (Mt.) or, in the plural, meticais.

6. The Government accepted from the outset of the ERP that the conflict would severely dampen responsiveness to the policy measures, but nonetheless considered that the establishment of an appropriate economic environment and appropriate economic policies were essential to take full advantage once peace was effectively re–established.

7. Data for the flow of financial aid, rather than these stock data, would have provided a more appropriate illustration, but they are not available.

8. There is little noticeable evidence of instability generated by non–RENAMO opposition to the FRELIMO Government. This, in principle, could have one of two causes: the absence of adequate political freedoms to express dissent or display destabilising behaviour; or the actual absence of any such tendencies within the opposition.

9. The aid was provided both in kind and through concessional finance.

10. Indeed, they will fall further if, as anticipated, South African immigration laws tighten.

11. These four periods were all post–Independence, post–exodus and relatively free from climatic trauma.

12. In this discussion of growth rates, it should be recalled that output was at exceptionally low levels.

13. Moreover, no data exist for foreign direct investment (FDI) before 1987, rendering impossible any analysis of private external capital flows, although it is doubtful that any significant FDI occurred.

14. To isolate the saving capacity of the domestic economy, one must exclude net external transfers from external savings (i.e. calculate the external current–account deficit before deduction of official external transfers). In Mozambique, this makes a major difference. For example, the external saving ratio in 1993 stood at 56 per cent excluding external transfers, but at 22 per cent including them. Moreover, rapid currency depreciation over the conflict period exaggerated the rise in all ratios with GDP as the denominator and with numerators that had significant external components. The local–currency equivalent of dollar–denominated external savings, for example, rose sharply as depreciation progressively reduced gross distortions in the exchange rate.

15. Official investment statistics define the sectors as essentially "Government" and "non–Government". Before economic reforms, substantial enterprises were in Government hands, so much of investment counted as "Government" was actually in state–owned enterprises (SOEs). Privatisations under economic reform during the third phase under review here have brought the figures closer to conventionally understood definitions, but four sources of distortion should be clear: (1) the commingling of enterprise and Government investment before reforms muddies the pre–reform picture; (2) SOEs, which had access to explicit or implicit Government subsidies, continued to invest in the pre–reform period with the support of external aid; (3) intertemporal comparisons are confused by changes in ownership (privatisation) in the reform period; and (4) the picture may remain muddied to the extent that privatisation is not complete. In general, if "private" investment as conventionally understood could be measured across the entire 1980–94 period, the divergences between "public" and "private" investment shown in Figure 2.5 would be even greater than they appear.

16. Some isolated, violent attacks continued, but they were interpreted as criminal, not part of any attempt to destabilise the peace process.

17. Recurrent budget outlays for the army (excluding the Ministries of Security and the Interior) were 5.1 per cent of GDP in 1993; they fell to 3.9 per cent in 1994 and about 2 per cent in 1995.

Chapter 3

Political Instability
in Post–Independence Zimbabwe

Introduction

The British South Africa Company colonised Southern Rhodesia (then the name for Zimbabwe) in 1890 and it became part of the Central African Federation established by Britain in 1953. Despite the discovery in the 1910s that it was not as rich in gold and minerals as initially predicted, the colony attracted significant white settlement in the early years of the century. Colonisers appropriated large amounts of land, including the most productive areas, and restricted Africans' access to productive assets and markets, limiting their activities to subsistence farming and labour. With the Unilateral Declaration of Independence (UDI) in 1965, Southern Rhodesia became known as Rhodesia under the white settler regime, and the Central African Federation dissolved when Northern Rhodesia and Nyasaland gained their independence. The United Kingdom and most other countries (except South Africa and Portugal) did not recognise the UDI's legitimacy and imposed severe economic sanctions against the Rhodesian Front (RF) Government led by Ian Smith. The RF nonetheless succeeded in retaining power from 1965 until 1978, continuing a severely repressive policy towards the African population that deprived it of political participation and economic advancement. An armed liberation struggle lasted almost a decade, intensifying after the 1974 coup in Portugal that ended Portuguese colonial power in southern Africa.

In 1978, internal settlement proposals devised by an interim Government of the RF and some minor, non–representative factions of the liberation movement including the United African National Council (UANC), were neither accepted by the Patriotic Front (PF) nor fully recognised internationally. The PF, formed at the instigation of the front–line states in 1978, was a coalition of the largest two parties in the liberation movement, the Zimbabwe African National Union (ZANU) and the Zimbabwe African People's Union (ZAPU). The non–representative character of the African element in the interim Government may actually have strengthened the PF's position, but any such effect became clouded and the unity of the PF threatened when Joshua Nkomo (the leader of ZAPU) entered into talks with the RF. In any event, the PF continued fighting until a final settlement came in the Lancaster House Agreement (LHA) of December 1979. The first democratic elections took place in 1980.

All parties in the region wanted a resolution. In the face of the escalating liberation war, the front–line states of Zambia, Mozambique and Botswana had suffered from Rhodesian cross–border raids and increased their pressure on the PF for a settlement, while the white communities in Zimbabwe and South Africa recognised the need to settle as the accumulated costs of the war mounted. The United Kingdom wanted an arrangement which compromised between the interests of African nationalists and those of the white community, and provided constitutional safeguards for the whites. The LHA in fact protected the position of the white community in the economic and, to some extent, bureaucratic structures in the post–Independence period.

The February 1980 elections drew 94 per cent participation; contrary to the expectations and hopes of the British and South Africans for a UANC victory, ZANU won 63 per cent of the vote, while ZAPU and UANC trailed well behind with 24 per cent and 8 per cent, respectively. Despite the constitutional safeguards, the victory of ZANU–PF caused immediate concern among the white community and led to further emigration, including members of the former Rhodesian army[1].

Following the LHA, the newly elected Government took a pragmatic approach of reconciliation and moderation in the design of economic and other policy. This delayed reform in some areas relative to the original hopes of the Government, notably in land reform and redistribution, but it had great success elsewhere. Important steps built up the institutional capacity of the country, decentralising the health administration, mobilising local participation and undertaking social investment in rural areas. Health and education spending as well as some infrastructure spending (especially transportation and marketing) helped to reduce perceptions of regional or ethnic segregation and to contain political pressures.

Continuing political instability in the early Independence period approached the dimensions of civil war but was relatively short–lived. It manifested itself in continued conflict between the two primary groups of the liberation movement, ZANU–PF and PF–ZAPU, which had formed the first post–Independence coalition Government, with ZANU–PF dominant because of its electoral success. Their falling–out intensified with the expressed intention of ZANU–PF to form a one–party state, a lack of political cohesion between them and alleged attempts to overthrow ZANU–PF. The coalition ended in 1982 with the forced dismissal of PF–ZAPU from the Government. In addition to creating regional and economic tensions, this political segregation of PF–ZAPU — the *Ndebele*–speaking group — provoked violent clashes in the PF–ZAPU stronghold of Matabeleland. The regional economic and political activities of South Africa further inflamed these internal disputes. In 1987, however, the conflict came largely under control, with ZANU–PF and PF–ZAPU again unified and a power–sharing Government established.

Hence, during the decade after Independence, the potential for political conflict between the white and African communities and within the leadership of the African liberation movement itself came largely under control, although outbreaks of social tension in the form of strikes and demonstrations continued even after the unification of ZANU–PF and PF–ZAPU. Social unrest resulted mainly from opposition to the Government's repressive policies, corruption and malpractice, and economic policies that brought significant reductions in social expenditure. The accumulation of financial imbalances from heavy social spending in the early years of Independence and significant increases in defence spending between 1982 and 1987 led to major cuts in social and infrastructure outlays in the mid–1980s. Discontinuity in some social programmes (e.g. health and education) and a lack of sufficient emphasis on employment–generating activities laid the foundations for future political opposition, especially in the growing urban population. In response to economic reforms and the emergence of better–organised urban interests, confrontations emerged between private entrepreneurs and rent seekers within the Government. They exacerbated tensions between ethnic groups, as minorities felt marginalised both politically and economically. So far, however, these events have not been sufficiently serious to pose a real threat to political stability.

Despite some policy weakness, therefore, notably a failure to institute major reform of the ownership structure, a degree of political stability apparently emerged. ZANU–PF gained an increasing share of the vote in the elections of 1985, 1990 and 1995. Yet this apparent stability was obtained in part at the expense of civil rights violations and other unpopular political practices which led to reduced electoral participation in much of the period.

Fundamental Determinants of the Political Environment

Four principal elements have determined the economic, political and social environment in the post–Independence period, and the capacity of the new Government to meet its objectives:

— the capacity to change the existing production and institutional structures and to implement redistributive policies while containing the potential for political conflict, particularly in light of the LHA and the safeguards granted to the white community;

— the inherited degree of inequality and dualism in the economic structure and its constraining impact on policies to enhance the degree of equity and avert political conflict;

— the presence of ethnic divisions; and

— the prevailing political and economic interests of South Africa.

The Lancaster House Agreement and Safeguards for the White Community

Independence in 1980 represented not an absolute transition of power from white–settler rule to African leadership, but a result negotiated under the chairmanship of the United Kingdom. As the prolongation of the struggle rendered a settlement increasingly compelling, the PF suffered a setback when many of the conditions agreed in the LHA did not accord it the outright victory it had sought. Some have argued that the ideological and political stance of the nationalist forces (mainly PF and UANC) was weak and the unified African leadership under the PF inexperienced when the negotiations were held. Although the nationalists had targeted the elimination of inequality, the colonial production system and its institutions saw no great challenge from the African parties due to the weakness of their programmes to restructure the economy systematically.

The LHA contained important constitutional safeguards for the socio–economic, political and military power of the white community with the stated objective of maintaining high efficiency and standards. Under the Agreement, the white community, only 2 per cent of the population, retained 20 of 100 seats in the Parliament. It received guaranteed protection from land expropriation for 10 years, except against acceptable compensation remittable abroad within a reasonable period. This specifically conflicted with a key objective of the liberation struggle, to reform the agrarian structure, as the cost of compensation would be very high and a major obstacle to reform[2].

The post–Independence Government adopted a philosophy of reconciliation and moderation as the basis for its strategy to overcome the potential for conflict between the white and African communities. In part, this approach necessarily reflected the constraints imposed by the LHA, but it also reflected the Government's genuine pragmatism in meeting the serious challenges to post–Independence stability. The institutions and structures of the colonial period and the circumstances that led to Independence largely shaped post–Independence social, political and economic relationships. Most significantly, the terms of the LHA constrained the redistributive capacity of the post–Independence Government by prohibiting of compulsory land expropriation from the white community. Its historical domination of the most productive areas of the economy, including high–potential land and much of the manufacturing sector, coupled with the lack of organised indigenous interest groups to present alternative development strategies, left the economic structure predominantly unchanged and the white community's share of total wealth disproportional to its population[3].

Forms of Dualism Inherited from the Colonial Period

Colonial rule had led to the concentration of economic activity in an agricultural sector that brought profitable rents, particularly following the Land Apportionment Act of 1930 which led to the appropriation of the majority of high–potential farming areas by the settlers. The land allocation gave them 51 per cent of the total land area and 78 per cent of the highest–grade lands, whereas most land allocated to Africans for subsistence agriculture in communal farming areas was of the lowest grades (75 per cent of the lowest grades were allocated to communal use). Moreover, irrigation, transportation and other infrastructural facilities were developed mainly for the high–grade lands occupied by the settlers for commercial use[4].

The UDI Government had adopted import–substitution strategies following the imposition of economic sanctions by the United Nations (UN) and the termination of trade with Britain. As a result, considerable economic diversification occurred; a highly capital–intensive industrial sector — mostly agro–industry — developed relative to other southern African countries (except for South Africa), paying higher wages than the agricultural sector[5] and accounting at the time for more than 30 per cent of GDP. Trade sanctions enforced the efficient use of blocked funds and the development of financial services. Agriculture remained important, however, accounting for about 70 per cent of the total labour force, 40 per cent of exports and 60 per cent of the inputs to manufacturing. Commercial farming employed about 35 per cent of the African labour force in 1977. With the mining sector largely foreign–owned, white commercial farmers were the dominant lobbying group and exerted monopoly power in setting agricultural prices through their influence on the marketing boards. As non–farm industry grew, however, urban consumer interests also gained importance.

At Independence, the economic structure discriminated heavily against the African community in terms of wages, employment and the ownership of land and other productive assets. An extreme duality characterised the agricultural structure, between sub–optimal production and overpopulation of the communal farming areas, with all their inherent environmental risks, and a large and mostly underused commercial farming area[6]. The white community owned most high–quality land and indeed still controlled 90 per cent of it in 1993. In manufacturing, whites owned most large–scale commercial enterprises while blacks dominated ownership of firms with ten or fewer employees. Wage and employment[7] policies equally discriminated against the Africans, with extreme wage disparities: at Independence, non–Africans earned 24 times the African wage in commercial agriculture, 7.3 times in manufacturing and

3.5 times in financial services (Fallon, 1987). In the public sector, few Africans held senior positions and only about 30 per cent of the lower–ranked positions were allocated to them.

Ethnic and Regional Divisions

Zimbabwe has two large ethnic groups, also distinguishable by language and region — the *Shona* and *Ndebele* — plus several minor ones. The *Shona*, about four times as numerous as the *Ndebele*, occupy the northern part of the country, Mashonaland; it has most of the high–potential land and most of the commercial farms (Table 3.1). Although it has only about four–fifths the area of Matabeleland, homeland of the *Ndebele*, commercial farms there had a share more than three times as large in 1979. In contrast, most of the communal land overused in subsistence farming lay in Matabeleland. Hence, in addition to the familiar forms of discrimination against the African community as a whole, Africans were also divided among themselves in access to potential wealth. The coincidence of Matabeleland and Mashonaland with the administrative boundaries and, more important, their highly differentiated land potential, have aggravated competition and conflict between the two ethnic groups both before and since Independence[8].

Table 3.1. **Regions, Rainfall and Farming Intensity**
(Percentages)

Distribution of Natural Regions by Administrative Areas	I	II	III	IV
Manicaland	17.0	5.3	42.4	35.3
Mashonaland Central		42.1	18.2	39.7
Mashonaland East		31.5	40.9	27.6
Mashonaland West		36.9	34.0	29.1
Midlands			64.2	35.8
Masvingo			14.9	85.1
Matabeleland North			6.2	93.8
Matabeleland South				100.0

Note: Ranking of natural regions is based on rainfall and farming intensity: region I has the most intensive farming and most rainfall, region IV the least. (natural regions IV and V are aggregated under IV.)
Source: Roth, 1994.

The independence struggle began with the formation of ZAPU in 1961; ZANU broke away in 1963. Although their leaders identified with the *Shona* and *Ndebele*, the distinctions were not originally at all well–defined; the founder of ZANU, for example, was himself raised in Matabeleland and had a *Shona* father and *Ndebele* mother. Whatever the role of ethnicity in the party leaders' real motivations, however, their followers divided mainly along ethnic lines. In the early 1970s, great disagreements

78

between the ZANU and ZAPU leaderships emerged and violent clashes erupted between their guerrilla forces. Each party often resorted to accusing the other of tribalism, which accentuated the ethnic element.

The emphasis on tribalism in explaining divisions in the independence movement stems partly from the two parties' lack of clear ideologies or sets of objectives. Divisions throughout the UDI period arose mainly from dissatisfaction with the leadership and disagreements over fighting strategy, as well as competition for power. Many military leaders and other Africans, including party and union leaders and intellectuals, suffered long exile during the 1970s, which led to some alienation from their popular bases. The guerrilla forces of ZANU and ZAPU (ZANLA and ZIPRA, respectively) remained somewhat detached from the political leadership[9]. In 1975, the front–line states helped to form the Zimbabwe People's Army (ZIPA), directed by a war council with equal membership from ZANU and ZAPU, in an attempt to overcome divisions in the movement and ensure a settlement. ZIPA soon disbanded, however, following clashes between ZAPU and ZANU forces over military strategy and leadership attitudes towards finding a settlement with the RF. Nonetheless, ZANU and ZAPU continued to represent the majority of the population. The failure of other internal African leaders, mainly the UANC, to secure a settlement with the RF in 1978 manifested this dominance of ZANU and ZAPU. The front–line states tried again to promote harmony with the formation of the Patriotic Front (PF) in October 1978, but the movement remained poorly unified when the settlement negotiations began.

The Impact of South Africa

Faced with the independence of several southern African countries and continuing guerrilla independence wars in several others, South Africa's interest in maintaining white dominance in Zimbabwe had grown greater than ever by the end of the 1970s. Besides political concerns, it considered maintaining the economic dependence of Zimbabwe crucial. It provided both financial and military support to the Rhodesian Government and its army, both to bolster them against the liberation movement and to sustain Rhodesian attacks on dissident elements and guerrilla bases in Mozambique and Zambia.

Throughout the 1970s and especially during the intense negotiations to reach a settlement, South Africa increased its military activities to weaken the struggle led by ZANU–PF, not only with support to Rhodesian forces but also by sending the South African Defence Forces (SADF) to infiltrate Zimbabwe in support of ZAPU against ZANU–PF. It also provided finance and training for the independent armed forces of Ndabaningi Sithole (former leader of ZANU), who was relatively better disposed towards South Africa[10]. The destabilising effects of South Africa's political and economic sabotage persisted after Independence, until the collapse of the apartheid regime in 1992.

Stabilising and Destabilising Elements of the Political Environment

The post–Independence Government faced the challenge of achieving growth and equity in a highly segregated socio–economic structure. In addition to the constraints imposed by the LHA to protect the white *status quo*, the trade–off gap between growth and equity loomed especially large due to the disparity in land potential of the regions inhabited by the two ethnically divided groups. Thus, two main types of potential political conflict threatened: that between the white community and Africans, and that among the Africans, divided by ethnicity, regional diversity and leadership. The integration of African and white representation into the political and economic structures presented the principal challenge in overcoming the first, given the institutional structure that had been shaped for decades under colonialism; here, the Government was largely successful.

The plans of ZANU–PF for a one–party state, the destabilising activities of South Africa and divisions rooted in the armed struggle for Independence all aggravated prevailing sensitivities related to the second type of potential conflict. The new Government initially emphasised the equal distribution of social spending in its development strategy. Education, health and some physical infrastructure spending increased substantially in the early years of Independence. Due to the minority position of the *Ndebele* and the army's legacy from the liberation struggle, coupled with the destabilising role of South Africa, political instability re–emerged after 1982. Only in 1987 did the violent confrontations subside with the unification agreement between ZANU–PF and ZAPU. The agreement included a commitment to establish a one–party state, which, even though it did not legally materialise, reflected Mugabe's desire to create a strong Government; with the help of repressive policies and a weak opposition, he largely succeeded in this objective. Since then, political instability has manifested itself in strikes and demonstrations by public workers and university students, sometimes backed by relatively weak African trade unions. They reflected worsening economic conditions, civil rights violations and inefficiency and malpractice in the Government.

To sum up, four major elements of the political environment contributed to stability or instability in the post–Independence period:

— the concessions to the white community;

— the relationship between ZANU and ZAPU;

— land reform and redistributive policy; and

— civil order.

Concessions to the White Community

Notwithstanding the LHA's protection of the white community's status, the ZANU victory in 1980 induced great fear within the community of instability under black African leadership. As a result, more white emigration added to the large number which had already left during the war in anticipation of a black victory. To counter this potentially serious loss, the Government immediately emphasised policies to reassure whites concerning both their economic interests and potential social unrest.

The justification argued that maintaining the white *status quo* for a limited time would aid an economically stable transition towards an African–dominated society and polity. The white community was in fact indispensable; it produced 90 per cent of the marketed food and most exports and inputs to manufacturing. At Independence, the State held only 16 per cent of productive capacity (excluding communal lands), while whites and Asians owned 28 per cent and foreigners the rest (World Bank, 1995*a*). The Africanisation of the state administration — including the parastatals and the University — in the early years of Independence did not demolish the position held by the white community; the rapid increase in the proportion of Africans in Government came without an excessive, substantive reduction of the white element, especially in the higher ranks (Table 3.2). Despite a brisk climb in the proportion and positions of Africans, the system retained many political and institutional elements of the colonial period.

Table 3.2. **The Distribution of Public-Service Employment**

	1980	1983
White	7 202	4 495
% of total	68	20
African	3 368	17 693
% of total	32	80

Source: Mandaza (1986).

The dominant view also held that the Africans did not have adequate experience or qualification immediately to take over commercial farming or industry. Thus white economic dominance continued and the inherited economic policies and institutions — such as pricing and marketing policy — saw no great challenge. At the political level, the ZANU–PF Government allocated the Ministries of Commerce and Industry and of Agriculture to white members of Parliament, and five other cabinet posts went to ZAPU[11]. The participation of black farmers in agricultural institutions such as the board of the Agricultural Marketing Authority rose, but the Commercial Farmers Union (CFU) maintained its dominant influence in agricultural policy. Final decisions on agricultural pricing shifted from the Agriculture Ministry to cabinet level, giving the Government more central authority while preserving the channels which transmitted the demands and expertise of the white community to the decision–making level. This policy effectively headed off the resentment of black farmers, despite continuing white influence.

Aside from the domestic economic and political reasons for reconciliatory policies, concern about the threat that South Africa could destabilise the regime unless the white community got sufficient concessions also had a role. Great economic dependence on South Africa (at Independence 90 per cent of Rhodesian trade went to or through South Africa, which provided 40 per cent of imports and took 25 per cent of exports) made the situation particularly delicate even after the lifting of the sanctions of the UDI period. Hence, the post–Independence Government gave great assurances to maintain the white community in order to avert any cause for South African retaliation. Nonetheless, the 1985 elections still reflected continued resentment by the white community; the majority of white votes went to the Conservative Alliance of Zimbabwe (CAZ), a party reconstituted from the RF under the leadership of Ian Smith. In retaliation, ZANU–PF allocated no cabinet posts to CAZ, but did nominate several whites to vacant positions. In 1987, it abolished (as permitted in the constitution) the reserved status of white parliamentary and senate seats.

The mining industry became a particular area of conflict between the interests of white settlers and the new Government. The post–Independence Government had identified it as primary for national development and had planned to nationalise the mostly foreign–owned mining companies, but abandoned nationalisation in view of the importance of foreign management and the sophisticated production linkages in the sector. It sought instead to control the marketing of mining output, creating a potential conflict situation, but then simultaneously reduced tension and facilitated its regulatory objective by appointing a white manager to the Mineral Marketing Board.

Although some tension remained between the African and white communities, the Government's power–sharing policies greatly eased the potential for political instability. After the expiry of the LHA in 1990, however, the Land Acquisition Act legitimised the compulsory acquisition of land by the state. This created some new tensions; arbitrary procedures for land acquisition brought adverse responses from the CFU and western donors, reflecting their concerns about the employment and investment that white commercial farming provided. Subsequently, however, the CFU assisted land reform and resettlement programmes, an illustration of the continued efficacy of the reconciliatory policies.

The Relationship between ZANU–PF and ZAPU

The guerrilla forces of the African liberation movement bore a high potential for political instability in the post–Independence period. Under the conditions set by LHA, ZANLA, ZIPRA and the Rhodesian army were unified to form the Zimbabwe National

82

Army. In the early 1980s, as a result of the emigration of many members of the former Rhodesian army and the breaking away of part of the former ZIPRA guerrillas, the ZANLA component came to dominate the Army. Moreover, former elements of the Rhodesian army which had remained in the country posed a threat as they continued to receive support from South Africa throughout the 1980s and had inherited the intelligence services of the former Rhodesian Government. Many who did emigrate joined the South African Defence Forces and continued to collaborate with their former colleagues in Zimbabwe. Some white civilians in Zimbabwe also supported activities to destabilise the new regime.

Although the new regime had broken diplomatic relations with South Africa in 1980, it did not terminate economic relations. Nevertheless, South Africa heavily limited Zimbabwe's trade and transit–trade activities, and initiated offensives along the Mozambique border, attacking black commercial–farming areas, infrastructure and development projects, as well as transport routes, petroleum facilities, ministerial residences and the air force. The attacks not only destroyed existing infrastructure but also increased the risk of new projects, thereby provoking a perception of Government neglect in the *Ndebele* region.

Although the *Ndebele* had fought more intensely in the liberation struggle, their smaller population compared to the *Shona* people left them at a disadvantage after Independence. Despite social and infrastructure spending in 1980 and 1981 which included Matabeleland, several factors caused an escalation of tension between the two groups. First, the *Ndebele* perceived further socio–economic discrimination by the Government, on top of repressive tactics already used to suppress political opposition. Second, droughts that hit Matabeleland severely in 1982 had a negative impact. Third, the destabilising efforts of South Africa and the former Rhodesian army elements bore some fruit. With the discovery of arms on ZAPU farms in Matabeleland and suspicions of ZAPU attempts to overthrow President Mugabe, the ZANU–PF and ZAPU coalition collapsed in 1982; Joshua Nkomo was removed from the Cabinet and his ZAPU colleagues dismissed from the Government and army. Some former ZIPRA guerrillas left the National Army in 1982 and, with ZAPU supporters, formed a major destabilising element in the western *(Ndebele)* region; severe conflict emerged between them and the National Army. Use of the armed forces in Matabeleland to control the escalation of violence further alienated the *Ndebele*–speaking population. These events sharpened the coincidence of party constituencies with regional and ethnic divisions, and ZANU gained no Matabeleland seats in the 1985 elections.

In response to the dissident activity and fierce fighting in Matabeleland as well as South African destabilisation efforts, ZANU–PF maintained repressive policies similar to those of the former white regime[12]. Unpopular practices such as press censorship and the empowerment of the security forces led to frequent detention and questioning of ZAPU officials, bans on public meetings and, finally, the closure of ZAPU party offices and district councils in 1987. Meanwhile, ZANU–PF increased its efforts to install a socialist one–party state and an executive system.

A major improvement in Matabeleland's security position came in 1988, after ZANU–PF and ZAPU unified to form a power–sharing Government under the title of ZANU–PF. Talks between the two parties had started in 1985 but suffered frequent interruption over disagreements on the allocation of Governmental positions. Another such break came in 1987, followed by a ban on ZAPU meetings, the closure of ZAPU offices in Matabeleland and intensified dissident activity in the region. Mugabe insisted that talks would not resume until the violence in Matabeleland was brought under control. The unification was finally agreed in December 1987, with a commitment to establish a one–party state. Under a revised constitution, the former ZAPU leader became one of the two vice–presidents under President Mugabe in 1989. Security in Matabeleland improved immediately after the agreement, supported by some successful social programmes in the region, such as decentralised health care. The end of the South African regime in 1992 and the cease–fire in Mozambique had a large, positive impact on the security of the entire region as well as in Zimbabwe.

Land Reform and Redistributive Policy

In line with its fundamental ideology and equity objectives, ZANU–PF's development plans targeted rural development, the improvement of communal farming and land reform, together with support for small–holder agriculture (albeit somewhat biased towards the high–potential areas). The Government also sought to make substantial improvements in the social conditions of the black community, and in fact achieved significant progress, especially in health and education. Due to a lack of available data on the regional distribution of communal and commercial land, not to mention the regional distribution of Government expenditure and investment, one cannot make precise judgements about the allocation of redistributive policies between the two major ethnic groups, but indications suggest that a significant share of drought relief and development funds was directed to Mashonaland[13].

Land has provided the essential source of political power and prestige for both the whites and Africans. The politics of land reform and analysis of resettlement tend to be obscured and complicated by the coincidence of regionally, administratively and ethnically segregated populations with the electoral bases of the two political parties. Arguably, one should more appropriately address redistribution from the perspective of the dualism between commercial and communal farming (Table 3.3), rather than from one of ethnic or regional segregation. White dominance on the land was defended mainly on the grounds of the indispensability of commercial farming because of its superior efficiency vis–à–vis communal farming, but this has been controversial. Indeed, with improved credit, market access and greater infrastructure spending during the early 1980s, communal farming significantly improved its market contribution[14], although long–term gains were limited by the overuse of land and associated environmental problems. Nonetheless, despite the safeguards of the LHA and the economic case for preserving the role of the white community, a resettlement programme was initiated. It funded agricultural and social infrastructure spending in targeted resettlement areas, but financial constraints in fact confined resettlement mostly to regions already relatively favoured.

Table 3.3. **Distribution of Farming Type by Natural Regions, 1988**
(Percentages)

	I	II	III	IV
Communal Areas	0.8	7.8	17.2	74.1
Large-Scale Commercial Farms	1.8	32.8	21.5	43.9
Small-Scale Commercial Farms	0.6	17.9	35.4	46.1
State Farms	2.0	2.0	32.0	64.0

Notes: Ranking of natural regions is based on the extent of rainfall and farming intensity: region I has the most intensive farming and most rainfall, region IV has the least. (natural regions IV and V are aggregated under region IV.)

Source: Roth, 1994.

Land reforms made gains after 1980 (Table 3.4) but fell well short of targets: by 1990, only 32 per cent of planned resettlement had actually taken place. The initial targets of 1980 foresaw large–scale commercial farmers giving up 57 per cent of their land to resettle 20 per cent of all the peasants between 1982 and 1985; a subsequent redefinition made this the final, overall target. The pace of resettlement dropped considerably after 1983, due mainly to the economic crisis resulting from drought but also to the political crises in Matabeleland and associated financial and institutional constraints. Moreover, earlier success in resettlement may mislead somewhat, because by 1989 half of the resettled farmers were squatters and much of the resettlement had taken place in Manicaland (bordering Mozambique), on land abandoned during the liberation war. In the early Independence years many of the resettled or squatters were former liberation fighters rather than communal farmers; resettlement was at least partly a form of compensation for their contribution to the liberation movement. The same occurred after the end of the hostilities in Matabeleland.

Table 3.4. **Shares in Total Agricultural Land**
(Percentages)

	1969	1993
Large-Scale Commercial Lands	50	35
Small-Scale Commercial Lands	0	4
Communal Lands	50	51
Resettlement Lands	-	10

The absence of the effective participation of local administrations in policy design has contributed to the lack of a well–defined resettlement procedure and effective regulation. This, coupled with the ability of squatters to benefit from loopholes in the central bureaucratic rules, put squatters in a much more advantageous position than communal farmers who lacked organisation and could not overcome the bureaucratic barriers that persisted from the former regime. The dominance of squatters over communal farmers in land resettlement illustrates the insignificance of ethnicity in the politics of land distribution, because no major divisions between squatters and communal farmers existed in terms of class or ethnicity. Indeed, this experience highlights the role (or the lack of it) of institutions in redistributive politics[15].

In general, policies to reduce rural–urban, communal–commercial and regional economic disparities have proved unsustainable. Throughout the resettlement attempt, especially in the early 1980s, commercial farmers continued to exercise major influence over agricultural policy decisions made primarily by the central Government. Despite some unfavourable international price movements, large–scale commercial farming has remained profitable due to a shift towards higher–value crops, greater product diversification and increased availability of foreign exchange since the late 1980s. Even after a significant reduction in the number of farms, large–scale commercial farming still occupies about one–third of all agricultural land (Table 3.4) and most high–grade land (84 per cent of the irrigated area and 59 per cent of natural regions I and II). Agricultural support services (marketing, subsidised producer prices) and credit directed to communal farmers and smallholders increased in the first half of the 1980s, but declined thereafter under fiscal austerity programmes, leaving the large–scale farming sector with growing output and employment while small–scale farming deteriorated. In 1990, the incidence of poverty still varied substantially; 40 per cent of the rural population (72 per cent of the total population) lived below the poverty line, as opposed to only 12 per cent of the urban population; and 58 per cent of Matabele South survived below the line in contrast to 23 per cent in Mashonaland East.

Despite the delay in land reform, no major political conflicts occurred. Weak local participation left white participation in agricultural policy unchallenged; while local administrations had autonomy in agricultural policy implementation, they got no participatory power in its design. This local weakness in the decision–making process has arisen from the lack of well–organised communal farmer interests; both the National Farmers Association of Zimbabwe (NFAZ), representing peasant farmers, and the Zimbabwe National Farmers Union (ZNFU), representing less productive, small–scale farmers in somewhat remote areas, have remained relatively ineffective.

Despite its failures in substantially reforming the inherited economic structure, the Government did implement many successful policies that helped reduce the potential for ethnic and regional conflict, especially through social services and the decentralisation of the state administration in some areas. Decentralising the health centres, for example, made the issue of health–service allocation a regional one, isolating central Government to a degree from regional pressures.

Another source of tension arose within the social structure. The expanding African *petite bourgeoisie* rapidly came to associate itself with the white commercial–farming and industrial interests that favoured existing mechanisms of allocation and distribution (including import controls, consumer subsidies, etc.). This arose in part from the prolonged economic and political deprivation during the Independence struggle, and in part from easy access to wealth and power after Independence. As the state sector expanded markedly, however, its rapid Africanisation and a highly controlled economy offered a convenient environment for rent–seeking activities.

After the unification agreement, social unrest appeared in recurrent strikes and demonstrations against reductions in social spending and repressive policies which censored the media, banned strikes and suppressed other democratic means of expression. The Government indefinitely extended a wage freeze put into effect in 1987, provoking many wildcat strikes, demonstrations and sit–ins. In 1988, Edgar Tekere, a former secretary–general of ZANU–PF ousted from the Government for corruption, formed a new party, the Zimbabwe Unity Movement (ZUM). ZUM's efforts, combined with student protests it helped organise, led to increased public opposition to ZANU–PF. The protests brought confrontations with Government forces and police, and resulted in closure of the University for seven months in one instance. Large–scale student and health–sector protests erupted in 1988, provoked by decreasing real wages and corruption scandals involving high–ranking Government officials that resulted in several detentions and arrests. The students called for nationalisation of the 80 per cent of the economy controlled by multinationals, freedom to strike and redistribution of land. In 1989, anti–corruption meetings and protests against civil–rights violations in the University resulted in violent clashes between students and police and, ultimately, closure of the University. When the Zimbabwe Congress of Trade Unions supported the student movement, its secretary–general was arrested. Media freedoms also suffered significant restriction in 1988–89.

Meanwhile, ZUM grew into the main opposition to ZANU–PF, obtaining 20 per cent of the vote in the 1990 elections, which were again marred by political violence. More student unrest followed in 1991. Several events linked high–ranking Government officials to corruption scandals. After enactment of the Land Acquisition Act of 1992, the first 98 farms acquired through compulsory purchases were leased to prominent party members rather than peasant farmers. These events served to exacerbate the prevailing public dissatisfaction, particularly with the lack of progress in land resettlement. Student protests persisted; in 1992, demonstrations against increased student fees and eroded grants resulted in 10 000 student expulsions, and in 1995 further student protests and violent clashes occurred over reduced and misadministered grants.

Mugabe's reconciliatory policies towards the white community seemed coupled with continuation of many repressive statutes and security institutions of the previous regime, and a continuing role for personnel like the police and former chiefs of the Rhodesian army. Some of these measures were repealed over time, but similar new ones gave the Government important discretionary powers. A feature of the institutional structure abetted such repressive policy: core executive agencies, rather than the legislature or judiciary, held most of the security powers. This apparatus, which ZANU–PF justified as needed to face South African destabilisation activities, provided the means to repress political opposition and restrict the civil rights of trade unionists, students and intellectuals. It also paved the way for a one–party state with increased centralisation of power. The 1990 elections saw continued repressive measures, such as restrictions on political speeches, assemblies and publications, which raised the inevitable question of how democratic the electoral process in fact was. President Mugabe went so far as to threaten civil service workers with dismissal if they voted for ZUM. Opposition to these tactics eventually led, in 1992, to the formation of the United Front (UF) against Mugabe among ZUM, CAZ and UANC. It failed to develop into a major opposition. Despite its attempt to discredit the Mugabe administration by not contesting the 1995 elections and disputing their fairness, voter turnout was 61 per cent and ZANU–PF received 82.3 per cent of the vote.

While these reactions have not yet presented any serious danger to political stability, repressive state policies did provoke, rather than suppress, the potential for continued unrest. Much distrust and resentment persist, between and among indigenous groups and non–indigenous ones with privileged positions in trade, between *Shona* and minority ethnic groups, between the political elite and the rest of the African community and, within the Government, between rent–seekers and those with market–oriented attitudes. In general, minority ethnic groups feel marginalised both politically and economically[16].

The Economic Impact of the Political Environment

The armed conflict in Matabeleland and dissident attacks on the Mozambique border proved extremely costly for post–Independence development. Particularly after 1982, the deterioration in the security position of the region and increased defence spending led to reduced Government investment in the productive, social and service sectors. Even after the situation improved in 1987, the state of emergency remained due to incursions in the east by RENAMO from Mozambique. Empowerment of the army and police force, together with the addition of new army brigades and the National Militia, to protect development projects led to increasing militarisation in the 1980s, constraining the development of a democratic environment. Government spending on defence remained at 6 per cent of GDP and between 14 per cent and 17 per cent of current Government spending in 1981–89, only a little lower than the corresponding figures of about 9 per cent and above 20 per cent, respectively, in 1980. By 1995, military spending had dropped below 5 per cent of GDP, but had not fallen much as a share of the budget. The share of defence spending in GDP and the number of soldiers per citizen remained higher in Zimbabwe than the African average.

South African attempts to destabilise the new Government proved especially harmful to land–locked Zimbabwe's trade through both South Africa and Mozambique. Both with threats to limit imports from Zimbabwe and by limiting credits for exports directed to it, South Africa aimed to dismantle the manufacturing sector and encourage the migration of skilled white labour to South Africa, intensifying the shortage of skilled labour in Zimbabwe. The share of Zimbabwe's exports going to South Africa fell from about 22.5 per cent in 1981 to about 9 per cent in 1990, while imports from South Africa fell from 27 per cent of total imports to 20 per cent. Despite the lifting of sanctions after Independence, Zimbabwe's trade showed no major improvement due to South African interference. After 1987, with the tightening of international sanctions against it, South Africa intensified its offensive on the trade routes of many southern African countries through Mozambique. Due partly to internal instability and partly to that elsewhere in southern Africa, Zimbabwe's exports fell from 30 per cent of GDP in 1980 to 27 per cent in 1984, while imports dropped from 33 per cent to 26 per cent. After 1992, democratic reforms in South Africa and more liberalised economic policies in the region stimulated both imports and exports, leading initially to a large current account deficit in 1992 that abated the following year (Figure 3.1).

Figure 3.1. **Imports and Exports** (percentage of GDP)

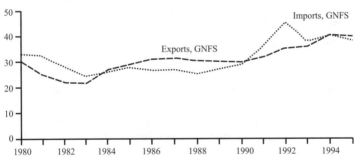

Increased Government spending on social services and infrastructure in 1981 and 1982 to reduce regional inequality contributed to success in containing ethnic–based conflict. Health, education and market–oriented infrastructure spending (especially on transport and local storage facilities) grew particularly in rural areas in the early 1980s; while disparities remained in health facilities, education services became broadly equalised between rural and urban areas. By 1990, Zimbabwe performed relatively well in many social indicators, as compared to both sub–Saharan Africa (except for secondary school enrolment and rural access to water) and other developing countries. Increased defence spending, however, coupled with a drought–induced decline in GDP in 1982 and 1983, led to reduced health, education and infrastructure spending in the second half of the 1980s. At this time, Government expenditures (including investment) still reached over 40 per cent of GDP, with defence accounting for more than 15 per cent of that[17]. Fiscal deficits, relatively high, averaged about 10 per cent of GDP in 1985–95, and the need to address this imbalance has often brought especially damaging policy reversals, notably in the health sector since 1992 (Figure 3.2).

Figure 3.2. **Fiscal Balances** (percentage of GDP)

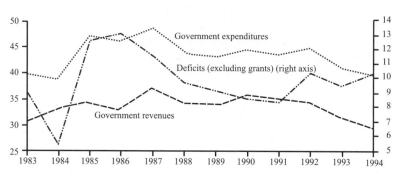

The Government's policy, especially its centralised approach to resource allocation, and the continuing dominance of white commercial–farming interests, kept both producer and consumer subsidies high in the early years of Independence. Agricultural prices were set in favour of the producers, because of both the influence of CFU (and the African farm unions that benefited from its existence) and the official objective of agricultural self–sufficiency. In the early 1980s, producer subsidies constituted about 46 per cent of total subsidies; consumer subsidies reached 20 per cent of the Government deficit in 1985. The manufacturing sector had become largely inward–oriented and capital–intensive during the UDI period, so controlled manufacturing prices and the allocation of credit and foreign exchange largely benefited large, established firms owned by the white community[18]. In the second half of the 1980s, large fiscal imbalances compelled the Government to reduce producer subsidies. Continued import–substitution policies and the protection of urban and manufacturing interests led to increased inequality and further potential for political instability.

The policies of the Government towards the white community produced no major economic restructuring, and the continued privileges of established white–owned enterprises in access to credit and foreign exchange necessarily inhibited the growth of small–scale black entrepreneurship. Despite some emphasis on decentralisation and community participation in social projects, decisions on planning, finance and allocation continued to be made in the central Government, as in the colonial period. Land–reform programmes were generally formulated on the same assumptions and methodology the Rhodesian Government had used, concentrating on the inefficiencies of land use in communal farming. This led to further state controls on tenure and land use. The eligibility criteria for settlement shifted from the landless and refugees to master farmers, which naturally favoured those who worked on established farms, on relatively good land. The resettlement areas were classified outside the communal farming category, and received even less security due to their greater vulnerability to political decisions. In the absence of any major organised opposition, these economic policies faced no serious challenge. Even after the expiration of the LHA, the pace of land resettlement remained slow.

The inheritance of a relatively more developed and diverse economic structure than was general in southern Africa helped the post–Independence Government to avert the major economic destruction that could have resulted from the destabilising effects of civil unrest and South African activity. After 1982, growth in manufacturing and mining did suffer from South African efforts to sabotage trade and transport. Some reform attempts in manufacturing had to be delayed, such as greater state participation in industry through the establishment of two parastatals, and self–financing structures for local authorities and agricultural marketing boards. Lower manufacturing input subsidies, part of reform programmes in the 1990s, led to discontent in the manufacturing sector; urban protest became increasingly vocal through the organisation of indigenous commercial and business unions in addition to the movements of civil servants and students. The economic reform programmes of 1994 aimed to extend foreign exchange availability and reduce protection to pave the way for manufacturing growth, including small–scale manufacturing, and thus provide new employment opportunities.

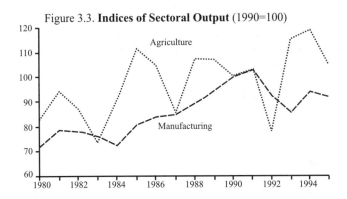

Figure 3.3. **Indices of Sectoral Output** (1990=100)

Most important, however, economic performance remains a major problem. Despite the significant effects of droughts, long–term trends in agriculture and manufacturing have pointed upward since Independence, but sluggishly, at average annual real growth rates between 1980 and 1994 of 2.5 per cent and 1.8 per cent, respectively (Figure 3.3). This performance has not met emerging needs. It has failed to generate productive employment opportunities in rural and urban areas. With rapid population growth of 3 per cent a year and growing urbanisation, the unemployed urban labour force has come to pose a major threat to social stability.

Notes

1. In 1975, the white population in Rhodesia was 278 000. By 1979 it had dropped to about 200 000. Heavy emigration after Independence left the white population at about 150 000.

2. The Agreement also included various provisions that guerrillas of the liberation movement should be isolated at assembly points designated by South African and RF intelligence, and thereafter integrated within the post–Independence army or demobilised. The PF was also unsuccessful in one other respect: its request for UN forces to supervise the transition, a reflection of its insecurity, was only partially met.

3. There was, however, a shift of lobbying power within the white community from the commercial farming sector towards the urban areas and especially the manufacturing sector, as reflected in policies for subsidies, credit and foreign–exchange allocation.

4. The distinction between communal and commercial lands is based on ownership rights: communal lands were historically controlled by traditional chiefs until Independence, when the Government took over the control of land allocation. Commercial lands, on the other hand, are subject to freehold tenure.

5. Average wages in the manufacturing sector were about four times those in formal agriculture.

6. Studies have found that 40 per cent to 45 per cent of the land in commercial farming areas was underused.

7. Labour mobility between farm and non–farm production was further limited by the recruiting of labour from other low–income countries in the region, such as Malawi and Mozambique.

8. Historically, both the *Shona* and *Ndebele* had further sub–divisions. Within the military hierarchy of the authoritarian *Ndebele* state before the colonial era, there were various castes, parts of which had *Shona* descendency. The *Ndebele* periodically raided the *Shona* chiefdoms. The *Shona* were even less united than the *Ndebele* due to different dialects and different chiefdoms.

9.   ZAPU and ZANU were financed by the USSR and China, respectively, and the influences of these separate ideologies aggravated the problems associated with the political divisions.

10.   South Africa was also allegedly involved in the attempt to assassinate Robert Mugabe (the leader of ZANU–PF) during the election campaign of 1980.

11.   The Minister of Agriculture was the leader of the former Rhodesian Farmers Union.

12.   A mainly *Shona*–speaking army brigade, formed in 1983, was particularly repressive towards ZAPU officials and their sympathisers in Matabeleland.

13.   In 1982, for example, the National Irrigation funds allocated to communal and small–scale farmers were completely used, and in 1989, 60 per cent of the Agriculture Finance Corporation loan for drought relief was allocated to Mashonaland with the remainder going to Matabeleland.

14.   In the first half of the 1980s, although still small in the budget, agricultural spending grew by 37 per cent.

15.   In Manicaland, where the majority of the squatters took root, alliances were formed with the ZANU–PF Government that enabled them to retain their dominant position in the resettlement process.

16.   In one gesture to counter continued signs of resentment by the *Ndebele*, Mugabe increased the number of *Ndebele* deputy ministers prior to the 1995 elections.

17.   In addition to the lack of resources, the threat of destruction by dissident attacks also contributed to reduced spending on rural development and infrastructure from the mid–1980s.

18.   Until the Economic Structural Adjustment Programme in 1994, Zimbabwe was one of the most highly protected economies in terms of tariff rates, price controls etc. (World Bank, 1995*a*).

Chapter 4

Political Instability in Zambia: 1964–96

Introduction

Northern Rhodesia's independence movement organised itself against the primary colonial objectives of economic and political integration with Southern Rhodesia and Nyasaland within the Central African Federation and with the other white minority regimes of southern Africa. Until Independence, Northern Rhodesia had played a particularly important role in providing the rest of the Federation, especially Southern Rhodesia, with resources emanating from its large copper mines[1]. In October 1958, the Zambia African National Congress (ZANC) broke away from the African National Congress (ANC) under the leadership of Kenneth Kaunda, in opposition to the ANC leadership's alleged accommodation to the British colonial order. With ZANC banned during violent unrest in March 1959 — which coincided with the declarations of emergency in Nyasaland and Southern Rhodesia — the United National Independence Party (UNIP) emerged from its lower ranks, again under Mr Kaunda's leadership[2]. Its increasing power, bolstered by that of the ANC, gave growing momentum to the movement for separation from the Federation, which culminated in national elections in January 1964. Victorious, UNIP formed the first African Government; Zambia thus obtained its Independence and ended its participation in the Federation.

Since Independence, the interplay of economic and political forces has twice led to political changes as the relative political power and position of the UNIP and the trade union leadership have changed, producing three regimes: the First Republic (1964–73), the Second (1973–91) and the Third (since 1991). Union labour constitutes the most organised socio–economic group. The UNIP Government has had regularly to deal with the power of the unions (especially during the Second Republic), sometimes through incentives and sometimes with repression. In addition, the political environment has strengthened the various organs of Government in ways which often produced opportunistic attitudes as officials used their positions to enhance their economic and social status. Political instability took the form of recurring struggle between narrow urban interest groups and the Government, which tried to implement national policies in the face of their often hostile opposition. Frequent outbreaks of unrest, including strikes and riots, posed problems for economic reform.

Box 4.1. Major Incidents of Political Conflict Since Independence

1965:   National strike by railway workers.

1966–67:   National miners' strike.

1968:   National strike by railway workers; ban on UP (*Lozi*–based); outbreak of violence in Copperbelt resulting in six deaths; ban on the organisation of the African National Congress in two areas where it had been strong.

1970:   National strike by teachers (last one before the ban on strikes).

1971:   University of Zambia closed for some weeks due to allegations against Kaunda about South Africa policy.

1972:   Single–party politics (ban on opposition parties).

1974 (Nov.): Substantial consumer price increases following World Bank recommendations (to reduce rural–urban disparities and to improve rural terms of trade by reducing agricultural subsidies, restraining urban wages, adjusting the structure of production and export incentives); led to demonstrations in Copperbelt and Lusaka, organised by ZCTU.

1980 (Oct.): Coup attempt by entrepreneurial group (businessmen, a high–ranking parastatal bureaucrat, a high–court judge), opposing Government for its inefficiencies in implementing development objectives; the six leaders of the coup attempt arrested and sentenced to death; the leader of the ZCTU, Frederick Chiluba, arrested on the grounds of attempts to overthrow the Government, later released as allegations were unsubstantiated.

1981 (Jan.): Strikes and riots in Copperbelt, 17 trade union leaders expelled from UNIP, then reinstated in April.

(July):   Further strikes, temporary detention of several union leaders.

1986:   Widespread riots following a 120 per cent increase in raw maize prices (15 dead, 450 arrested) led to reintroduction of the subsidies.

1987:   Protests in Lusaka, forcing Government to cancel 70 per cent increase in fuel prices.

1988:	Coup plot (army officers and civilians), in which Kaunda alleged the role of South Africa and some other foreign countries.
1989:	Riots in Copperbelt due to increase in maize prices (reintroduction of price liberalisation); demonstrations by University students.
1990 (June):	Violent riots (50 deaths) provoked by the austerity measures, and strikes led by unions demanding multi–party democracy; a false Government take–over announced on the radio by a junior army officer, leading to demonstrations in celebration of the end of Kaunda's regime.
(July)	Lifting of 17–year ban on organised opposition groups, announcement of referendum for transition to multiparty democracy.
1991:	Violent clashes between the members of MMD and UNIP prior to the first democratic elections in two decades.
1992:	Widespread opposition to the MMD Government's reform policies; clashes between students and the security forces.
1993:	State of emergency following the discovery of UNIP documents concerning destabilisation of the Government; arrest of the three sons of Kaunda, subsequent release of two and retention of the third (the leader of the military wing of the UNIP).
1995:	Arrest and later release of Kaunda on charges of illegal meeting prior to by–elections.

The main potential threat to political stability has changed over time. During the First Republic, the chief source of social unrest lay in the desire of the indigenous population to catch up with the living standards of the whites; the already organised trade unions demanded large wage increases as compensation for their role in the independence movement, at the expense of national equity objectives. The UNIP established a one–party system to deal both with this inconsistency between powerful union demands and its national objectives and with the increasing strength of opposition movements. Having exploited the resources of the highly productive copper industry to boost wages, consumption and imports during the First Republic, the Government faced increasingly frustrated demands during the economic downturn of the Second, when copper revenues plunged. Bad economic management, which made the economy highly susceptible to economic shocks, and repression in response to the threat of instability, reinforced and unified organised opposition to the UNIP Government.

Growing domestic and international pressures forced the Government eventually to organise multi–party elections in 1991, which marked the beginning of the Third Republic. Given the economic problems and anti–democratic practices associated with UNIP during its two decades in power, the newly elected party, the Movement for Multi–Party Democracy (MMD), initially enjoyed popular support and backing from the international donor community in undertaking its programme of economic reform, despite evidence from the 1980s of considerable implementation difficulties. Although the Government pursued market reforms much more decisively during the 1990s, public reaction to reduced real wages, unemployment and official corruption grew. Although the 1990s seem relatively more stable due both to an improved regional environment and to a relatively more democratic regime, lack of significant economic recovery has turned initial public support away from the MMD towards an increasingly fractionalised political opposition.

Fundamental Determinants of Political Instability

Post–Independence political conflict in Zambia had its roots partly in the dual economic structure of the colonial period. The colonial regime's emphasis on copper development bifurcated the economy into the relatively modern mining sector with its supporting activities, and the rest of the economy, left practically untouched. Cheap labour came from emigration of the rural population to urbanised mining regions. In the transition to Independence, the political environment changed. A mass movement based on widespread demands for independence and racial equality evolved into internal political conflict between those espousing national objectives and the interests of organised socio–economic groups. To see how this came about requires analysis from four perspectives: first, the role of the strong trade unions in the Independence movement and their continuing strength after Independence, particularly in pressuring the Government to accelerate redistribution; second, how the dual economic structure caused organised interests to emerge; third, the ideology and objectives of the post–Independence Government, and how they became potentially contradictory in implementation; and fourth, Zambia's ethnic structure.

Role of Labour Unions

In the 1930s, employer–employee relationships and the representation of African workers began to evolve from tribal and generational bases. The formation of African trade unions became legal in 1949. The African Mineworkers Union (AMU) originated from within the branches of the European Mineworkers Union (EMU), despite EMU efforts to prevent an independent African union. Both the white workers' unions and the prevailing structure of the transportation and communication networks facilitated the development of the African labour organisations around the copper mines and their distribution zones.

Under colonial rule, a dual wage and employment policy paid the whites — around 15 per cent of the labour force and 40 per cent of them South African — according to European standards; Zambians received much lower wages. Top management and supervisory positions went almost exclusively to the white settlers, reinforcing the disparity. In the 1950s, European workers but not Zambians benefited greatly from bonuses based on copper–price increases; this generated a more vocal resistance to racial inequality. The AMU organised strikes in 1952 and 1956. Rioting occurred in 1958–62[3]. Although African wages improved considerably, the differential remained very high; in 1960, the average wage of European mineworkers was about nine times that of African ones (Table 4.1). The almost homogeneous position of the Africans, consistently paid much less than whites and consistently held to lower–ranked positions in the mines, facilitated union organisation. Exploiting the common interest in equal employment conditions for Zambians and whites, the AMU started to organise further strikes and riots that became a contributory force in the moves towards Independence.

Table 4.1. **Average Annual (Kwacha) Wages in 1960**

	Agriculture	Mining
Zambian	120	570
Non-Zambian	2 406	5 188

Source: Zambia, Central Statistics Office.

Occupational Segmentation

The copper mines have long provided the major economic activity; in 1964, copper production accounted for around 40 per cent of GDP and 90 per cent of export revenues[4]. It provided about half of formal–sector employment in the 1960s and closer to 60 per cent in the 1970s. Until 1969, Roan Selection Trust and the Anglo–American Company, mainly financed from the United States, the United Kingdom and South Africa, owned the mining industry. Independence did not immediately lead to a change in ownership until the programme of nationalisation was established towards the end of the 1960s. Nevertheless, the strong position of the mineworkers as both a large political power base for the UNIP Government, especially in the Copperbelt region, and the labour force in this core economic activity gave them considerable leverage in pressing the Government to accommodate their wage demands after Independence. Economic conditions during the First Republic, namely the copper boom of the second half of the 1960s and the early 1970s, favoured a positive Government response.

Contrary to conditions in mining that favoured and encouraged formation of effective interest–group coalitions, the agricultural sector could not organise effectively. The vast area of arable land, relatively sparsely populated rural areas and the lack of well–developed transportation and communication facilities all weakened political mobilisation. Moreover, the rural class, about 70 per cent of the population in 1960, and especially agricultural labour, never felt exploited in the absence of a widespread landlord–peasant system. Rural labour was neglected in the emphasis on industrialisation objectives. Thus, the cheap, urbanised labour force in the mining sector became the closest candidate to represent the peasant/worker class. The political parties made no rural appeals because few in the political elite had rural backgrounds. This duality eventually became a major source of political conflict by enhancing the power of the mineworker unions in opposition to more comprehensive and egalitarian national policies[5].

Ideology and the Objectives of the UNIP

UNIP's fundamental ideology was African Socialism, which sought to promote African advancement and racial equality while welcoming private entrepreneurship. The UNIP Government came to power with two objectives: Zambianisation or African advancement, and the acceleration of economic growth and productivity. With insufficient qualified African personnel, however, a legacy of the colonial period, they proved inconsistent. Better–trained and experienced European settlers continued to hold many of the key managerial positions. In consequence, the Government's emphasis on copper revenues as the engine of growth, coupled with its lack of adequate administrative capacity to effect major policy change, led to significant continuation of colonial production relationships in the early years of Independence.

As widening economic disparities appeared among the Zambians, the Government placed increasing emphasis on Zambian Humanism, under which economic equality became the principal objective of national policy. As the Government attempted to increase its administrative control over implementing this policy, a new Zambian middle class emerged. Moreover, competition for power within the ranks of Government intensified as the attractiveness of becoming a bureaucrat or politician earning a relatively high salary increased. Nevertheless, at this early stage of Independence, amidst favourable economic trends and the reduction in racial tension, none of these developments threatened instability.

Ethnicity

Before Independence, sectionalism based on linguistic and provincial differences presented no potential threat to political stability, due to an absence of tribalism and, more important, the unifying force of opposition to the prevailing racial discrimination on both political and economic grounds. Ethnic groups in Zambia were not effectively organised. Indeed, the presence of 73 ethnic groups and some 80 rural groupings speaking different languages — none of which constituted a majority — operated as a natural barrier to the formation of such coalitions. Language defined groups better than regional boundaries. The single largest such ethnic group was the *Bemba* (18 per cent of the population) of the Northeast and Copperbelt regions, followed by the *Tonga* of the Southern Province (10 per cent), the *Nyanga* of the Eastern Province and the *Lozi* of the West.

Although diverse ethnicity *per se* did not lead to political instability, opposition groups that emerged in the post–Independence period exploited ethnic differences in the struggle for power. UNIP drew its initial electoral base mainly from the *Bemba*–speaking Northern and Luapulo provinces, whereas the earlier roots of the independence movement in the ANC had support chiefly in the *Tonga*– and *Ila*–speaking agricultural populations in western and southern areas. UNIP organised its militant movement in the mining areas of the Copperbelt region mainly to take advantage of organised mineworker union power; here, the *Bemba*–speakers dominated. The UNIP leaders' alleged favouring of this group in the subsequent distribution of Governmental posts became one of the reasons for political opposition towards the UNIP leadership, notwithstanding that *Bemba*–speakers perceived themselves as under–represented in key party posts relative to their contribution to the independence struggle. Political conflict based on sectionalism thus emerged over competition for privileges associated with high Government rank, a phenomenon irrelevant in colonial times. The dual economic structure also led to perceived discrimination among regional groups not on the major trading routes.

Post–Independence Sources of Political Instability

Zambianisation and Resulting Social Segmentation

The UNIP Government pursued Zambianisation by advancing Zambians into managerial positions, with a first focus on positions in personnel administration. The dominance of European employees persisted to some extent, however, as noted above. Zambianisation often led to the creation of additional layers of management, and thus to reduced efficiency. New Zambian managers also became more conscious of differentials in wages, benefits and authority *vis–à–vis* European supervisors, especially within the higher ranks of the mining hierarchy and in comparison with Europeans in similar management positions. Under the old regime, one could at least explain discrimination by the different positions held by black and white workers.

In 1966, the Brown Commission's look into wage differentials between African and non–African workers led to the unification of pay scales, with the wages of mineworkers subsequently increased by one–third in real terms by 1967 and by a further 15 per cent by 1975. While this accommodation of demands generated a potential for wage–driven inflation, wage differentials between the whites and Africans were greatly reduced, thus meeting one of the main objectives of the independence movement. In fact, this transformation during the First Republic had no serious economic impact because the extremely strong performance of the copper industry provided the necessary financial resources.

These changes did, however, intensify the duality in the economy. The powerful Copperbelt trade unions had already pushed Zambian wages in the mining sector higher than the national average; in 1964, a Zambian miner earned an average wage about five times that of a Zambian in agriculture (Figure 4.1). This rural–urban inequality improved only slightly as the ratio declined only to about 3:1 by 1975[6]. It not only led to increased migration to urban areas, where the major copper mines were located, but also spread wage increases to the rest of the formal sector, because private and parastatal firms largely shared the same benefits.

Figure 4.1. **Ratio of Average Annual Wages Between Sectors and Racial Groups**

Annual wages (in current Kwachas)

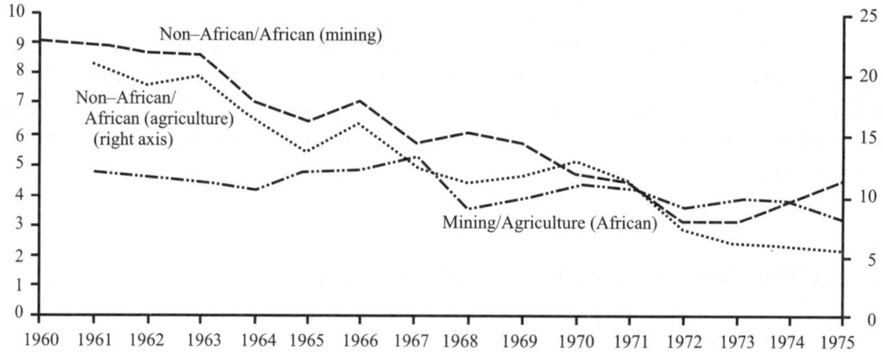

The main targets of national economic policy sought growth through higher productivity and reduced inequality through economic diversification. The unions came to assume a dual role, representing national policy on the one hand, and the workers' objectives on the other. At the same time, increasing differences emerged between the upwardly mobile managerial class and the common mineworker. Rapid Zambianisation of the mines produced an upper class of Zambians who associated themselves mostly with the Government and conformed to national policy, leading, for example, to their siding with the Government in response to union strike action. In return, they were typically rewarded with incentives such as high–paying Government jobs. The more qualified local union leaders often had opportunities to work in the mining companies too. With these possibilities of upward mobility, the union leadership increasingly aligned itself with the Government and the companies themselves, and this generated a tension between the mineworkers and their Zambian supervisors[7].

The emphasis on copper revenues as the main resource to finance development led to increasing official involvement in mine management. The Government tried to use the union worker representatives to implement its objectives against the narrow wage interests of the workers. UNIP's policy to reconcile these two potentially conflicting interests focused on seeking voluntary labour participation through incentives, and by allowing mobility towards Governmental positions and promotions through the productivity councils. Thus, a prime role in promoting national development objectives came to rest with the union leaders, who progressively hardened their stance towards the mineworkers. The miners' reaction appeared in increased numbers of offences, absenteeism and reduced productivity. Moreover, as European managers, fearful of losing their positions, became more cautious in interacting with local workers, Zambian supervisors became perceived as much tougher. On balance, rapid Zambianisation in fact led not to conflict between Europeans and Zambians, but to strife amongst the Zambians themselves.

The trade unions had only a weak practical capacity to perform as intermediaries for the Government in imposing production objectives in the mines. They could not but respond to increased demands for equal wages which brought strikes and subsequently wage increases. Meanwhile, Zambianisation of management targeted only egalitarian and humanitarian objectives without much regard to efficiency and optimisation goals, because the new middleclass of Zambian managers/bureaucrats did not have skills equivalent to those of the white managers. Thus, although the objective of reducing racial inequalities was largely achieved in the mining sector, objectives of management and productive efficiency were not.

Nationalisation and Increased State Control

The inconsistency between accommodating urban wage demands and the national objectives of increased equality and productivity finally led the Government to implement its economic policies more aggressively. Nationalisation of the copper mines and the major companies, therefore, came partially as a response to urban resistance towards its policies. Moreover, the emergence of a dominant new Zambian managerial class (see Box 4.2) had its roots not in the colonial past but in this nationalisation at the end of the 1960s.

The UNIP Government launched the Mulungushi Reforms in 1968 by partially nationalising some commercial and industrial enterprises. In the copper industry, the foreign companies which hitherto had controlled production and investment had mostly expatriated the sector's profits during the copper boom. Given the importance of the industry for foreign exchange revenues and its share in fiscal revenues, the Government in August 1969 requested the two main mining corporations, NCCM and RCM, to offer 51 per cent of their shares to it (the Matero Reforms). Despite this change in ownership, many expatriate managers remained in place, in the absence of educated

Zambian substitutes with appropriate technical skills. The Mining and Industrial Development Co–operation (MINDECO) was established to control the sector, and the Industrial Development Corporation (INDECO) was enhanced to promote new industries and control the partly nationalised firms.

President Kaunda used state control to institutionalise his policies and increase their effectiveness directly by prohibiting strike action and repressing opposition to them. The Government created about 80 parastatals in the ten years after Independence, ensuring its control by appointing their management and using incentives to ensure loyalty. This extension of Government ownership signalled the beginning of a state–capitalist phase in the Zambian economy, creating a bureaucratic and managerial structure that led directly to confrontation with labour militancy. Government appointments to top posts in INDECO and MINDECO brought increased dissidence by local union leaders against the national leaders.

The Government also attempted in the 1970s to rationalise the industrial sector to enhance efficiency, a need which became pronounced with the collapse of copper revenues after 1975. Yet nationalisation, the principal policy, proved very costly, with compensation to the former company owners typically financed by bond issues or foreign borrowing. It had two primary beneficiaries: the foreign companies, which received very generous settlement payments, and the mineworkers, who benefited in the short term as state participation allowed mines to survive that would not have done so under strictly commercial conditions.

In 1980, NCCM and RCM, the two largest mining companies, were merged to form Zambia Consolidated Copper Mines, Ltd. (ZCCM), with the Government's share increased to 60 per cent. Opposition even from within the Government appreciated the risks involved with this merger, among them the possibility that this large conglomerate could exercise excessive influence on the rest of the industry, especially through its ability to direct resources in pursuit of particular strategies.

Corruption

As a result of Zambianisation and especially nationalisation, personnel loyal to the party mostly filled the higher ranks of the hierarchical structure. Indeed, such loyalty became a more important criterion for appointments than skills and ability. These personnel received relatively good salaries as an incentive to promote Government policies, with civil servants in the higher ranks earning as much as 20 times as those in the lower ranks[8]. The creation of this large bureaucratic structure bred increased incentives for corruption and favouritism.

The first inquiry into alleged malpractice, undertaken in Zambia Railways in 1977, revealed evidence of corruption, tribalism and nepotism. In 1978, investigation of selected parastatal companies led to the discovery of large losses associated with administrative malpractice. In general, Zambians' lack of experience in administrative bureaucracies and the shortage of skilled personnel help to explain the escalation of administrative malfunctioning and the opportunities created for corrupt activity. With deteriorating economic conditions, inefficiency and corrupt practices in the higher ranks of the state administration intensified, provoking a coup attempt in 1980 and an increasing strikes in the 1980s[9].

The Corruptive Practices Act of 1980 offered a response to growing administrative malpractice, but incidences of corruption continued, leading to further hostility to the Government and increased threats of political instability. As public reaction to the economic reform programmes and administrative deficiencies grew in the 1980s, UNIP suffered a significant loss of political support. Meanwhile, the Government continued its anti–democratic policies, not only controlling the press, but also declaring most strikes illegal.

Theft and similar crimes also increased substantially in society at large, notably in the early 1980s. The increasing number of urban unemployed and a stock of guns left behind by the Zimbabwean freedom fighters contributed to the escalation of crime, while the security forces remained understaffed and ill–equipped to deal with it, often being themselves corrupt.

The One–Party State

Post–Independence political competition for economic power and influence was often based on regional and linguistic segmentation. A major ideological difference within the Government related to the administrative style of the party; while *Bemba*–speakers generally favoured a populist, mass–participation approach, the *Lozi*–speakers (generally younger and more educated) favoured centralism. In general, however, attempts to explain post–Independence and indeed pre–colonial political conflict, or simply political alignments, from a purely ethnic perspective fail for lack of any consistent patterns. Despite frequent coincidence of ethnic and sectional differences, post–Independence political conflict stemmed mainly from competition for higher–ranked political and bureaucratic posts rather than historical, ideological or ethnic roots. Emerging political groups or parties did, however, frequently make various groups believe incorrectly that they were discriminated against by the Government.

In any event, increasingly serious cleavages emerged: between common mineworkers and union, company and state–sector management; between the union leadership and the Government; between factions within the Government; and between the Government and its shifting opposition. In consequence, the post–Independence political situation displayed on–going instability, ranging from worker slowdowns to coup attempts.

By the late 1960s, the Government started to become increasingly non–accommodative and more repressive. President Kaunda put a ban on ANC party activities and, following clashes in the Copperbelt, on the United Party (UP), which had been formed among the *Lozi*–speaking ANC and members of the UNIP. Tribal connections or language–based segregation characterised most of the factions within the Government; this intra–party conflict led in 1971 to the formation of the United Progressive Party (UPP) by *Bemba*–speakers in the Copperbelt. The Government detained some 100 UPP supporters and increased its repressive action, while at the same time extending large salary increases to public workers and the armed forces to prevent further defections to the UPP. The shift of political support to the UPP in the Copperbelt cost UNIP most of its private–sector support among farmers, business and the unions. Concerned that it might lose the Copperbelt and Northern provinces to the UPP and become a minority party in the 1973 elections, the UNIP Government banned the UPP in 1972, making UNIP the only legal party. In order to overcome factionalism in the Government and seize greater political control, Kaunda increased his presidential powers, leading to a changed constitution and a one–party participatory democracy in 1973.

106

After constitutionally eliminating all the opposition, Kaunda became the sole presidential candidate in the elections of the 1970s and 1980s, and was elected with an increasing proportion of the vote, accompanied by a dramatic decline in voter participation. UNIP policies still met increasing challenge within the Government as a more educated group replaced former local party leaders in the National Assembly. The potential for conflict came mainly from two political groups: the more business–oriented technocrats, such as the managers of parastatals, and national politicians still attached to humanitarian objectives of equality. In addition, economic decline affected the real salaries of the armed forces and raised tensions between the army and the Government; coup attempts in 1980 and 1988 reflected this uneasiness between the Government and the army.

In the 1980s, the Government reacted to union opposition by making great efforts to extend its control over the economy. Bad economic management and political repression, however, led to increased pressure from business, farmers and trade unions, as well as from within the UNIP, to transform the political system. By the end of the decade, both donor organisations and Zambians had lost confidence in UNIP's ability to implement reforms and effect an economic recovery; they became increasingly more organised against it. In March 1990, President Kaunda organised a conference on political and economic reform, hoping to mobilise political support and strengthen his position. It failed in this purpose, and a referendum on the future political structure emerged as the most legitimate solution. The imminence of a fundamental political restructuring became increasingly apparent when demonstrators took to the streets to celebrate a false coup announcement by a junior army officer in June 1990. In November, Parliament unanimously passed the Constitution of Zambia Amendment Bill to allow the formation of political parties, partly in expectation of increasing the UNIP's legitimacy. A new constitution was adopted in August 1991, with President Kaunda acceding to the MMD's demands to exclude provisions on presidential power to impose martial law and appoint ministers only from the National Assembly.

The MMD's victory by an overwhelming majority in the 1991 elections lent strong initial support to economic reform. The new Government launched a comprehensive programme to spur economic growth by emphasising reduced state intervention and more market–based and efficiency–oriented policies. IMF and World Bank recommendations formed the foundations. Their conditions, mostly met, led to price liberalisation and subsidy reduction, but also increased unemployment and an appreciated real exchange rate.

Allegations of corruption and malpractice nonetheless continued. Many cabinet reshuffles reflected the difficulties of maintaining a team to undertake and ensure the continuation of the reforms, but on balance the first half of the 1990s saw a relatively more liberal environment than before for political participation, a freer press and a more stable economy as budget deficits and inflation fell back. High unemployment and accumulated imbalances from many decades of economic mismanagement continued to pose many challenges for sustaining both economic reforms and political stability.

Other interest groups have not counterbalanced the economic and political power of the mining sector. This has left the Government unable to create the necessary support for reform policies geared to economic diversification, and in turn has increased the potential for political instability by reducing the prospects for growth.

Prior to Independence, many European farmers left the country in anticipation of land nationalisation. That did not immediately occur, but the new Government did limit remittances abroad and, as policy focused mostly on redistribution towards the mining sector, agricultural pricing and marketing policies failed to provide incentives to farmers. Moreover, land incentives provided by the white–minority regimes of southern Africa encouraged white emigration. Hence, expatriates in agriculture decreased further, from 16 per cent of the farm labour force in 1964 to 3.5 per cent in 1983. Moreover, while commercial farmers had relatively easy access to credit, small ones typically could obtain short–term loans only against crops, not other collateral. In fact, the credit system was particularly cumbersome because land effectively had no value other than that of improvements on it. Many attempts at agricultural reform in the late 1960s and early 1970s failed to make any significant progress; the focus remained on industry–based growth and import–substitution policies. Farm production became dependent on foreign finance. Meanwhile, despite exchange controls, large European commercial farmers mostly expatriated their profits.

The land–tenure system has also contributed to the lack of incentives to improve productive efficiency in agriculture, and thus to its continuing disadvantage and the widening gap between the rural and urban populations. Commercialisation by settlers had taken place mostly on freehold crown land along rail or trade routes, but the Land Act of 1975 made these lands (6 per cent of the total) state land, offered to the public under leaseholds with 100–year terms. Moreover, while the lack of a differential rent system had generally led to an under–used[10], large–scale form of commercial agriculture, the weak institutional capacity of land administration further reduced security of tenure and therefore long–term investment.

At the start of the 1980s, the Government introduced a plan to establish large state farms, mirroring the parastatals of the industrial sector. Like the Zambianisation of the copper mines, this resulted in reduced efficiency on commercial farms because the country lacked the required capital and Zambians the appropriate training. In 1981, the Government adopted a less interventionist rural development policy, focusing on infrastructure, rural services and promotion of commercial farming by Zambians. The National Agricultural Marketing Board (NAMBOARD), created in 1968 to centralise marketing and distribution and operating mainly along the rail lines, was replaced by Provincial Co–operative Unions, which showed little additional success due to the lack of an educated agricultural labour force.

Thus, policy weakness persisted, with no effective rural development policy. To avoid the high political cost of upsetting urban consumers, the Government heavily subsidised agricultural consumer prices, particularly for maize, which continued to undermine farm development. These subsidies began in 1970 and claimed growing shares of Government expenditures (Table 4.2). Thus, despite its objective of equitable development, the Government ended up protecting urban consumers at the expense of the unorganised farmers. Producer subsidies for maize and fertiliser mostly benefited commercial and medium–scale farmers, and hampered incentives for diversification into other, drought–resistant crops. Efforts from the late 1960s to mobilise agricultural investment funds through co–operative movements failed, principally from a lack of education and administrative capacity. Fixed investment in agriculture, already very low during the First Plan (1966–70), dropped further, from 5.2 per cent of GDP in 1971–75 to 3 per cent in 1975–80. Credit and marketing policies failed to provide sufficient incentives for new commercial farmers. Agricultural production remained mainly in the hands of small and medium–sized private holders and the reduced numbers of expatriate commercial farmers who remained.

Table 4.2. **Maize Subsidies**

Year	% of Government budget
1980	9.3
1981	6.3
1982	8.4
1983	8.4
1984	5.5
1985	6.1
1986	10.5
1987	10.9
1988	16.9
1989	16.1
1990	13.7

Relations between UNIP and ZCTU

The involvement of labour in management began when UNIP established the Zambia Congress of Trade Unions (ZCTU) in 1964, to centralise the labour movement and control it within national policy. Wage, Price and Productivity Councils also were established to provide productivity incentives and control unjustified wage increases. Local union leaders, however, typically former pre–Independence leaders not appropriately educated to represent the union, generally were excluded from the decision–making processes. Increased control in the management of the nationalised sector came with the Industrial Relations Act of 1971, which unified the labour movement under the central regulation of the ZCTU. It replaced voluntary participation with more repressive policies, effectively making strike actions illegal by establishing lengthy conciliation procedures. In principle, it provided for local Workers' Councils to enhance labour participation in implementing national policy, but management usually set the meeting agendas and workers had little real power over decision making[11].

Figure 4.2. **Strikes and Real Wages**

Source: ILO various years, and Rakner (1992).

Deteriorating economic conditions and tighter union organisation due to the Industrial Relations Act led to greater homogeneity among union workers and union managers. As real incomes deteriorated towards the end of the 1970s and trade unions became more confrontational, the Government moved to increase its administrative control. The Local Government Act in 1981 sought "decentralised centralism" by strengthening local Government administrations and replacing mining township authorities. Union opposition to this loss of control in the mining townships resulted in dismissal of several MUZ and ZCTU leaders by the Government and subsequent industry–wide strikes. Although the leaders were later readmitted to the UNIP, relationships deteriorated and some union leaders were arrested for several months. The ZCTU's opposition to the one–party system and the UNIP administration became aggravated as economic conditions worsened and the Government made further attempts to assimilate union power in 1982, 1986 and 1990. Strikes (both the number of days lost and the number of strikes) correlated inversely with real wage trends (Figure 4.2).

Hence, rather than suppressing labour power, official attempts to centralise production decisions both financially and organisationally strengthened union organisation under the ZCTU. A ZCTU leadership change in 1974, in favour of a liberal candidate, Frederick Chiluba, reflected this. Union support moved away from UNIP as the ZCTU reacted increasingly to Government efforts to suppress union autonomy and became the focus of opposition to the Government. By 1980, the ZCTU had 16 affiliated unions, including the MUZ which represented the Copperbelt mineworkers; ZCTU membership reached 80 per cent of formal–sector employment. The major political opposition to the UNIP in the late 1980s continued to be organised around the ZCTU, culminating in Chiluba's formation of the MMD in 1990.

To summarise, the policies of the UNIP Government empowered the unions not only by emphasising copper revenues and rapid Zambianisation of the mines, but also through increased state control and repressive policies that followed the economic downturn. The downturn had itself reduced real incomes and eliminated the rents previously appropriated by organised labour, resulting in more strikes and demonstrations. The emergence of a technocratic middle class with different perspectives on national policy than that of the UNIP Government further entrenched opposition to it.

Deterioration in the Terms of Trade and the Policy Response

The economy deteriorated sharply in the mid–1970s, as violence and conflict increased within and between the political parties, between trade unions and the Government, and between the white–minority Governments of the south and the Zambian Government. Although rooted in structural factors, the economic decline stemmed from a severe deterioration in the terms of trade. Sharp falls in copper prices and a persistent decline in copper production drastically reduced copper revenues by the end of the 1970s. The copper price plunged in 1975 and continued to fall until 1987, returning to its 1975 level only in 1989, while copper output also dropped steadily to only about half its 1970s level in the 1990s (Figure 4.3). Droughts that led to large losses of agricultural output between 1979 and 1984 and again in 1992 and 1994 reinforced the economic slump.

Figure 4.3. **Copper Output and Prices**

Copper production and real price

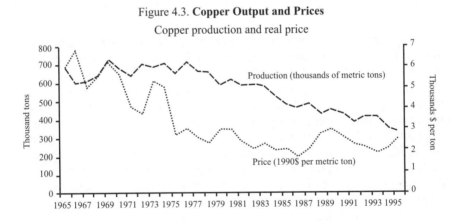

111

The fall in copper revenues turned out to be much more persistent than initially predicted, seriously impeding the economy's import capacity. Imports fell to half their 1975 level by 1987. During the First Republic boom, import dependency had grown and become entrenched. Buoyant copper–export revenues went neither to reserve accumulation nor to investment in economic diversification, but instead to imported inputs for capital–intensive investment and imported luxury goods for consumption by the Zambian elite. These policy failures aggravated the economic downturn, as import dependency led to a substantial deterioration in fiscal, domestic and foreign savings, and in investment (Figure 4.4). Fiscal balances deteriorated particularly sharply because taxes on copper had accounted for 53 per cent of aggregate Government revenues prior to the downturn.

Figure 4.4. **Consumption, Investment and Domestic Savings** (percentage of GDP, 1977 Kwachas)

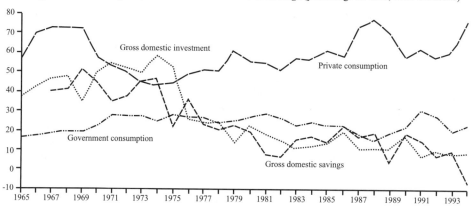

In response, the Government adopted a series of economic reform programmes sponsored by the World Bank and the IMF, with stand–by agreements in 1973, 1976, 1978, 1983, 1984 and 1986. Each such effort typically focused on securing fiscal balance by reducing subsidies, increasing maize and fertiliser prices, restraining wage growth and imposing new taxes. Exchange–rate adjustments[12] and liberalisation of foreign exchange and credit policies also had prominence[13]. World Bank and IMF programmes proved short–lived, however. The agreements of the 1970s were completed, but all those in the 1980s were interrupted or cancelled due to the eruption of political conflict, primarily over real–wage declines in the face of rising inflation (Figure 4.5). Debt–rescheduling agreements with the Paris Club and bilateral donors could not prevent further accumulations of arrears and increased future debt–service obligations.

Each break in the reform programme brought important policy reversals. They typically involved quantitative restrictions on imports to protect an overvalued exchange rate, along with administrative allocation of foreign exchange. Credit rationing tried to contain current account deficits, despite the increasingly inefficient resource allocation it created. With an overvalued Kwacha (despite several devaluations) foreign exchange reserves fell, and administrative controls only bred a fertile environment for favouritism and corruption.

Per capita income has almost halved in real terms since Independence (Figure 4.5) because population growth has exceeded real economic expansion. While the decline resulted chiefly from inefficient resource allocation and exogenous factors, the nation's lack of human capacity has functioned importantly as both cause and consequence of the deterioration in economic performance. The paucity of skilled labour created an obstacle to designing and implementing effective development policies. Although school enrolments rose substantially between 1964 and 1978 — by 155 per cent in primary schools, 520 per cent in secondary schools and 336 per cent in technical schools (ILO, 1981) — educational resources did not get increased proportionally and the quality of education fell.

Figure 4.5. **Trends in Per Capita GDP and Inflation, 1965-1995**

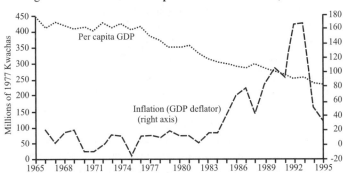

In addition to problems created by declining revenues and prior policy mistakes, public management decisions during the downturn did not reflect economic priorities and ministries did not co-ordinate. While the Ministry of Finance managed current budget balances, the National Commission for Development Planning (NCDP) tried independently to achieve the plan targets for investment. With the IMF stand–by agreements of 1976 and 1978, the positions of the Ministry of Finance and the Central Bank progressively strengthened. As a result, the Government focused current spending cuts disproportionately on capital expenditures to control sharply increasing budget deficits, thus heavily impacting on agricultural development, education and health spending.

The relatively high wages of formal–sector employees, reflecting the buoyancy of industry and their bargaining power until the early 1970s, had to be reduced after the 1975 downturn. The decline in real earnings, including those of the public sector, by almost 40 per cent between 1975 and 1989 led to mounting cleavages between the trade unions and the Government. Formal–sector labour became more united in its opposition to Government policy and the reform programmes. In this painful process, income distribution did tend to equalise; the ratio of average wage earnings in mining to those in agriculture fell to 1.50 in 1986 from 4.43 in 1970 (Figure 4.1). Informal–sector wages were even lower, at less than half of formal–sector wages.

Having become a more encompassing organisation representing wider economic and political interests, the ZCTU established itself as an effective challenger of the UNIP. It advocated structural adjustment, including lower parastatal subsidies, but criticised the Government's approach and the harshness of the IMF reforms. Although large devaluations could have increased export competitiveness, they did not prove practical in the nexus of domestic and global economic problems; rising import prices from devaluation would especially have harmed the urban lower and middle classes.

Increased dissatisfaction with the Government led to further reductions in productivity and escalating violence. In December 1986, the abolition of maize subsidies and a more than doubling of the maize price caused large and violent demonstrations in major urban centres. The Government then withdrew the price increases and nationalised the maize mills. Large declines in employment and real wages in the service sector also provoked severe labour unrest at the beginning of 1987. A foreign–exchange auction mechanism introduced in 1985 to replace the import licensing system had led to some correction of the much–overvalued Kwacha (to K15=$1 from K2=$1). This auction mechanism was suspended in 1987, in a bow to heavy opposition. A two–tier auction system followed, in which foreign exchange only for Government and debt–service transactions and agricultural inputs could trade at a first auction window, and only within a band of K9 to K12 to the dollar. When the value of the Kwacha fell to K21=$1 at the second window, the Government abandoned auctions and reset the value at K8=$1. Devaluations through the auction mechanisms never approached a market rate, but did help mining and some import–substitute industries. The party elite and administrators suffered, especially as travel and luxury consumption goods increased in cost. This intensified opposition from within the bureaucratic class, former Government members, businessmen, army officials and the trade unions.

The Government then embarked on an Interim National Development Plan that targeted growth and low inflation and distanced itself from the donor community by limiting debt payments and fixing the exchange rate. This programme also failed to reduce maize subsidies and inflation; as living standards further deteriorated, the UNIP was compelled to restart negotiations with the IMF in 1989. The new IMF programme again entailed devaluation and price liberalisation. Further riots erupted and the ZCTU broke from the UNIP. Although the MMD supported the IMF programmes, it found that the situation considerably enhanced its power. This paradox arose from its close links to the ZCTU, which had long positioned itself against the UNIP policies that led to real wage reductions and overall economic decline, and which had been excluded from decision making on the reform programmes.

Violent clashes between the MMD and UNIP ended in 1991 with the transition to multi–party democracy and the assumption of power by the MMD. In its own response to the economic crisis, the MMD immediately launched another comprehensive economic programme. Such were the unrealistically high public expectations and the unfeasibility of meeting them quickly that, after an initial phase of public support, fiscal austerity once again produced increasing opposition, new parties and ethnic and regional fractionalisation. Allegations of malpractice also became a major factor. The security forces continued to play a role in repressing public opposition to the reforms.

Regional Conflict

Since Zambian Independence, neighbouring countries have had serious political turmoil at one time or another — liberation struggles in Mozambique (1964–74), Angola (1961–74), Zimbabwe (1965–78), Namibia (1966–88) and South Africa, and civil wars in Angola (1975–92), Mozambique (1975–92) and Zaire (1964 and 1978). Zambia's ideology defined its role in the region as a front–line state against repressive white–minority regimes. It played an active role both in the various peace initiatives in the region and in support of the ANC after it was banned from South Africa as well as the PF in Southern Rhodesia. Zambia accommodated refugees from Zaire, Angola, Zimbabwe and South Africa, and provided a base for many of the liberation movements in the region, thereby remaining vulnerable to the attacks of the white–minority regimes of southern Africa.

The country's land–locked position made it particularly vulnerable to political developments in neighbouring countries, including serious distortions in trade, transport and communication facilities. Traditional export routes for copper ran mainly through Rhodesia to South African and Mozambican ports, and through Angola *via* the Benguela Railway. After the UDI in Southern Rhodesia, the new Tazara Railway was built through Tanzania, both as a reaction to the closure of the Southern Rhodesian border and to reduce dependence on southern routes[14]. The cost of liberation wars and rebellions around the region has been very high. Estimated costs to transport copper increased from K64.2 per ton in 1969 to K108.7 in 1979. The conflict in Mozambique cost Zambia an estimated 20 per cent of its GDP by 1988. Exports to Southern Rhodesia halved after the closure of trading routes in 1965; but shipments to Zimbabwe quadrupled in 1981, the year after its Independence, suggesting the possible magnitude of Zambian exports forgone before then.

115

Violent attacks which often occurred towards the end of the 1970s prompted the Zambian Government to increase defence spending; by 1980 it accounted for around 15 per cent of GDP and over 30 per cent of total Government expenditure. Such spending, combined with reduced import demand from neighbouring states, had severe economic costs which exacerbated the domestic political pressures faced by the

Government. By 1990, defence spending had fallen back to about 4 per cent of GDP, but it still took about 29 per cent of Government current expenditures (US ACDA, 1994/95). In 1993, the corresponding figures were about 2 per cent and 25 per cent.

Aside from the economic costs — especially the destruction of its few trading routes and tourism earnings — and outright attempts at destabilisation from South Africa, already described in another context, political conflict in southern Africa sometimes was reflected in Zambia's internal politics. When President Kaunda's secret communications with South Africa in 1968 and 1969, aimed at securing peace settlements for the independence movements, were exposed in 1971, his opponents accused him of collaboration with South Africa. In January 1976, students demonstrated in response to allegations of the Zambian Government's support for the Angolan Government (UNITA) against the Marxist MPLA movement, and of collaboration with South Africa in an abortive intervention. The demonstrations resulted in arrests and the University's temporary closure. The private sector and its representatives in the Government opposed UNIP's policies of disengagement from the south through the closure of the trade routes; a former vice–president (Kapwebwe, the former leader of UPP) was imprisoned for such dissent.

Medium– and Long–Term Prospects

Economic Prospects

Economic policy to sustain political stability must focus on management of the current internal and external balances and the external debt; high debt resulted from the vicious circle of political conflict and poor economic policy, reinforced by the vulnerability of the economy to exogenous shocks. Since economic recovery is essential for political stability, and political support is necessary for the sustainability of restructuring policies, the potential for future political conflict is associated closely with the ability of the Zambian Government to implement its reform programmes. External aid plays a very important role in providing social safety nets necessary to avert the tensions likely to emerge during economic restructuring.

The debt burden increased after 1985 to unsustainable levels as domestic and external imbalances accumulated, leaving Zambia one of the most highly indebted countries in the world. By 1995, the debt–service ratio had reached 42 per cent, with the debt stock at 193 per cent of GDP. Servicing it necessitated credible reforms to maintain much–needed flows of foreign financing. Donor support fluctuated with the reform efforts, however, although it has increased throughout the 1990s. Technical assistance, more concessional debt (100 per cent in 1991–93), debt buy–back operations and reschedulings provided by international donors have turned debt flows and transfers positive since the 1980s. Short–term relief from reschedulings, however, has not reduced the long–term debt burden, leaving a pressing need to address long–term questions of export capacity and import dependency.

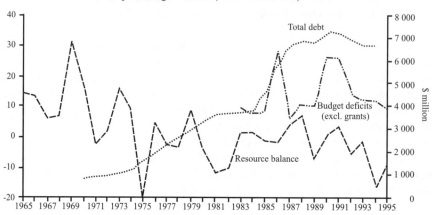

Figure 4.6. **Internal and External Balances and Foreign Debt**
In percentage of GDP (current Kwachas)

Along with continuing privatisation[15], budgetary performance should further improve with the fiscal reforms under way. They include the introduction of a cash–budget system to restrain expenditures, a VAT to expand the tax base, treasury–bill auctions to reduce reliance on the Bank of Zambia, and the suspension of ZIMCO. The inflation rate, which closely reflects the stability of the fiscal accounts, dropped from above 100 per cent in the early 1990s following the onset of price liberalisation to about 30 per cent in 1995. Reduced pressures for monetary expansion and inflation have helped to build the credibility of the reforms, as increases in the flow of external grants confirm. Yet the success of fiscal reform hinges crucially on the maintenance of social safety nets to cushion the costs of adjustment. Without such support, it is difficult to see how the Government can establish the all–important political support. Sustained external support and directing resources to employment–generating activities seem essential to avoid future political conflict.

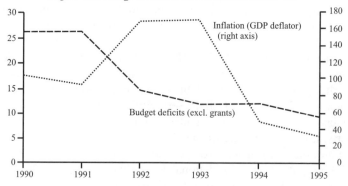

Figure 4.7. **Budget Deficits and Inflation: 1990–95**

Reliance on a single export commodity for economic growth points up the need for economic diversification. While the rehabilitation of copper production, requiring substantial restructuring and investment in both old and new mines, should produce some medium–term recovery, policy design must reflect the economy's comparative advantage and the realities of land–locked Zambia in a region dominated by South Africa. Although unorganised and long subordinated to industry, agriculture has potential. Failure to develop it has contributed to political instability both by causing increased migration to urban areas and by lowering the economy's growth potential. With a large area of unfarmed arable land[16] and relatively good weather conditions, agriculture offers considerable promise for economic diversification — for its own sake and to create new support groups for economic reforms, an important step towards greater stability. Given increasing demand for food and regional conditions, agro–industry and small business in Zambia could play a leading role in economic growth, provided that investment gets channelled towards drought–resistant crops. The incentive structure for private investment also depends on improvements in financial intermediation.

Zambian businessmen supported MMD primarily for its promises to increase trade with South Africa and implement policies encouraging foreign investment. The economic reforms of the 1990s have tried to keep them. Positive support from the international financial institutions has helped provide the Zambian economy with much–needed funds to initiate economic diversification and efficiency–enhancing liberalisation measures. Agricultural policies since 1991 indicate a gradual transition towards decontrol. Although it is too early to measure the results, an increasing share of private and smaller–scale marketing and trading operations, as well as a shift away from maize towards other marketable agricultural or agro–industry production, are positive steps in promoting economic diversification.

Political Prospects

From the political–economy point of view, the 1990s resemble the Independence period in some key ways. Paralleling the success of the UNIP in the 1963 elections, the MMD won the 1991 elections by a sweeping victory (with 83 per cent of the vote, although the participation rate was very low at 45 per cent). Dissatisfaction with UNIP among MMD leaders provided the primary unifying force behind the victory, but the party owed its formation to the wide trade–union power of ZCTU, whose leadership reflected a broad regional and occupational diversity, including the newly emerging middle class, technocrats, academics and businessmen. Balancing these different interests appears difficult. It has raised questions of favouritism in appointments[17] to managerial and Government positions. Continued division within the party and the emergence of many new parties mirror developments in the immediate post–Independence period; three new parties have emerged from within the MMD, led by dissident ministers of the new Government. The main causes again seem to have their roots in the unequal treatment of different groups, as well as the reaction to alleged malpractice and corruption within the Government.

Although the MMD has advocated multi–party politics, it apparently has favoured transformation to a single dominant party once again. A constitutional provision, not revised since the 1970s, which gives more power to the President than to the executive, contributes to these concerns. As the UNIP experience showed, a single big party may itself weaken the democratic process and promote political instability. Indeed, in order to eliminate UNIP opposition in the 1996 elections, MMD sought a constitutional amendment to render Kaunda's candidacy illegitimate for his failure to register at Independence as a Zambian citizen. Such attitudes, coupled with continuing economic difficulties, have contributed to an increasing potential for political unrest, at least among the reviving ranks of UNIP supporters.

Concluding Remarks

Throughout the post–Independence period, Zambia has struggled to transform its long–repressed political and economic system into a more liberal one. The lack of administrative experience and the shortage of appropriately qualified personnel, coupled with the dual economic and social structures, largely account for the problems that have plagued the establishment of a democratic environment and efficient markets. Although many of these obstacles go back to the colonial inheritance, the mismanagement of economic policy since Independence has exacerbated them.

Nationalisation and Zambianisation policies aimed essentially to wrest productive assets and their management from the white settlers. Yet they produced a large and inefficient state sector, increased controls and a new class of Zambian beneficiaries from the prevailing, even aggravated dualism. When the economy turned down, these new factors all contributed to the emergence of political conflict, so it would be wrong to attribute all the reform failures to inherited problems. The failure of the First Republic to exploit favourable initial conditions with a well–designed growth strategy reflected economic mismanagement as much as the inherited lack of qualified personnel. Excessive reliance on copper revenues and weak diversification policies made the economy highly vulnerable to severe, negative external shocks. Political reform was equally weak; the one–party system and the Government's repressive tactics during the Second Republic delayed transition to a more liberal structure.

Nevertheless, this experience contributed to an increasing desire to re–establish multi–party politics and generated increased support for economic reforms. After many years of growing opposition to a Government identified with economic decline and political repression, the multi–party democracy since 1992 has given the incumbent party a chance to implement reforms. Like its predecessor, it has found it more difficult to change economic and institutional structures than to mobilise political opposition — and Zambia now has a large industrial and urban population that can organise relatively more effectively than in the past.

The significant role of organised opposition groups, especially trade unions, stems partly from the colonial period. It has created large–scale social tension that has played a big part in the largely peaceful political and economic transition of recent years. Overcoming the dualistic structure of the economy demands an interest–group diversity that can overcome the too–few dominant groups of the past and support economic reform programmes geared towards long–term, economy–wide benefits. As compared to the 1970s, Zambia now has an array of agricultural and business lobbies, with at least a potential for maintaining a democratic environment.

Notes

1. The British South African Company (BSAC) had taken control of the mines, Northern Rhodesia's main industry, by obtaining the mineral rights in 1891.

2. After separating from UNIP, the ANC maintained its power only in the Southern and Central provinces; UNIP's strongest support was in the Copperbelt region.

3. Some 37 riots were recorded during this period.

4. By 1995, the share of copper had declined to about 10 per cent of GDP, starting with a severe drop in 1974, and about 70 per cent of export revenues, the result of a more gradual fall since 1974.

5. Not unlike the agricultural sector, the manufacturing, construction and trade sectors were also organisationally weak and geographically widely scattered, while the financial and service sectors were only a little more organised.

6. The increase in the urban proportion of the population to more than half in 1990, as compared to only 24 per cent in 1964, underscores the growth of the urban poor.

7. In total, the supervisory positions in the mines accounted for one–tenth of the labour force, and of these one–third were in the union leadership.

8. Earnings in the rural areas, on the other hand, were even lower than those of the lower–ranked civil servants.

9. The students of the University of Zambia also demonstrated against the inefficiencies in university administration, resulting in the closure of the University by the Government for several months.

10. Zambia has a vast arable land area, but a utilisation rate of only about 10 per cent.

11. In May 1976, Workers' Councils were relaunched in an effort to introduce greater industrial democracy with worker participation in management.

12. Devaluations in 1976 and 1978 amounted to a cumulative 20 per cent depreciation in the value of the Kwacha.

13. As part of the copper rehabilitation programme, a serious restructuring of ZCCM occurred in 1986, sponsored by the World Bank, with 4 000 workers laid off.

14. South Africa provided a significant part of Zambian imports: about 15 per cent at Independence, declining to 5 per cent in 1974 and rising to 20 per cent or more in the 1980s after a relative improvement in regional trade relations. Zambia spent a large proportion of its budget to delink itself from South Africa by building other routes, due both to its opposition to the South African regime and to the obstacles to copper exports created by regional instability.

15. As of 1996, 15 out of 80 parastatals had been privatised.

16. Only 6 per cent of potentially fertile land was cultivated in 1990, due partly to the controls on agricultural prices.

17. The senior executives in the parastatal organisations were mostly replaced by the new Government.

Chapter 5

Determinants of Political Stability in Botswana: 1966–96

Introduction

When Botswana obtained Independence from the United Kingdom in 1966, it was one of the poorest countries in the world, with a per capita income of $95. The discovery of diamond mines at the end of the 1960s, however, dramatically changed its course; by the 1990s, Botswana had become the second–largest diamond producer in the world and joined the lower middle–income group of countries. Over the past 30 years, the real growth rate of domestic output has averaged more than 10 per cent a year, 7 per cent in per capita terms. In 1992, per capita GDP reached $2 775, ranking second on the continent to South Africa's $2 951. Since Independence, Botswana has enjoyed notable political stability, maintaining a multi–party system and fair democratic elections.

Pre–Independence Elements of Political Stability

That Botswana inherited no major ethnic rivalries and economic dualisms at Independence constitutes the most crucial characteristic of an economic and social structure which has enabled political stability. In addition, it obtained Independence peacefully, with British agreement and with no major conflict between its *Batswana*[1] and expatriate populations. The economy, small and underdeveloped at the time, remained highly dependent on the United Kingdom and South Africa for aid and trade. The post–Independence Government, formed by the Botswana Development Party (BDP) with British support, represented a continuation of the previous administration. It posed little threat to the status of the expatriate community and adopted moderate foreign policies which made it less subject to regional political pressures.

The mere absence of special–interest group pressures does not sufficiently explain the country's political stability because it begs the question of why it appeared. Underlying socio–economic structures and policies crucially determine interest–group formation. Moreover, if economic stability is a precondition as well as an outcome of political stability, the determinants of economic stability also need analysis. Botswana has had good governance as well as good fortune. Diamond revenues have enabled the Government to prevent socio–economic pressures from arising by providing a share of the growing pie to the rural poor in the form of safety nets against drought. Government policies, combined with resource availability stemming from favourable exogenous factors, have helped inhibit the emergence of powerful opposition. Three central factors brought this about: political development before Independence; the absence of significant socio–economic dualism; and no ethnic conflict.

Political Development

Northern Bechuanaland became a British Protectorate in 1885 and remained so until Independence in 1966 when it became Botswana. The British established the Protectorate mainly to secure trade routes between central and southern Africa, threatened by an expanding German presence in the west and the Portuguese in the east. The struggle with the Germans and the Boer settlers over trade, especially after the discovery of gold in the 1880s, provoked Britain to take the step. It ended prolonged uncertainty about incorporating Bechuanaland into the Union of South Africa. At the time, the British Government, unwilling to assume the costs of administering the Protectorate, intended to hand over administration to the British South Africa Company (BSAC). It dropped this proposal in 1895 as a result of the on–going Anglo–Boer conflict and lobbying against the BSAC by chiefs of the three largest *Tswana* tribes (Khama of the *Ngwato*, Setshele of the *Kwena* and Bathoen of the *Ngwakeste*).

Britain administered the Protectorate from the southern region, known as British Bechuanaland before its subsequent incorporation into the Cape Colony. The Protectorate did not even have a capital until shortly before Independence, reflecting the colonial power's fundamental lack of interest in Bechuanaland itself. Indeed, it exercised control through the traditional chiefs, thus making them a part of the administrative bureaucracy. This enhanced the chiefs' authority within the traditional structures, relative to the *kgotlas*, the tribal assemblies or village forums that constituted the outer circles of the traditional concentric power structure[2].

At Independence, 40 per cent of GDP arose in agriculture, traditionally the main economic activity. Although Botswana has a large land area, only about 1 per cent of it is fertile and that remains vulnerable to extreme drought[3]. More than 80 per cent of the population lived on subsistence farming, yet only 5 per cent of the total arable area was cultivated in 1965. Cattle ranching, the main domestic activity generating foreign exchange, provided the economic basis for a relatively powerful political elite;

tribal chiefs and foreigners generally owned the large cattle herds. The chiefs' economic power therefore rested on two foundations: their status as cattle owners, and their collaboration with the colonial power, which included a privileged and sometimes abusive role in tax collection[4].

With the British Government unwilling to meet the costs of administration, domestic taxes became the most important revenue source. These revenues came mostly from customs duties and regressive poll taxes, the more important of the two, which in some years reached 60 per cent of total revenues. Poll taxes also became significant for wealth distribution and labour mobility. Until 1966, the British Government provided some additional revenue through aid grants; begun in the 1930s only to compensate for the loss of cattle export revenues following the interruption of trade with the Union of South Africa at the time, they increased somewhat in the 1950s in an ineffective attempt to make up for past neglect.

In consequence of its lack of natural resources and resulting colonial negligence, Botswana had only a very poorly developed social and physical infrastructure prior to Independence. The colonial administration left such investment to the tribal authorities and missionaries. It provided no funds for Africans' primary education, for example, causing it to vary greatly in quality depending on differences in revenues raised locally. Europeans and Africans had very unequal access to social infrastructure; in the early 1930s, hospital–bed ratios amounted to one per 250 Europeans and only one per 2 800 Africans (Colclough, 1980). Agricultural and physical infrastructure suffered similar neglect; roads remained largely limited to the towns and the single railway served only the eastern part of the country. Veterinary services, however, received between 10 and 15 per cent of public revenues because of cattle exports' importance to the revenue base. Benefiting both European and African cattle owners, they constituted the single most important benefit provided by the colonial administration. The British Government attempted to improve the social infrastructure in the second half of the 1950s, but its aid grants were too small and too late. Nevertheless, the education and health indicators had improved somewhat by Independence, to levels exceeding the average for low–income southern Africa.

The colonial era ended without a fight. During the transition between 1961 and 1965, the Botswana People's Party (BPP) had emerged as the main liberation party, with a political philosophy inspired by the ANC in South Africa and by a fundamental antagonism towards colonialism in general and the racially based South African regime in particular. It had remained prone since establishment, however, to many divisive splits within its organisation. As a result, Seretse Khama, with the support of the British Government, formed the more moderate Botswana Democratic Party (BDP) in 1962. The British and South African Governments as well as the *Tswana* chiefs favoured the BDP over the BPP due to both its democratic, non–racial stand and its promise of a constitutional role for the chiefs[5]. The first democratic elections, in 1965, gave the BDP a victory with 80 per cent of the vote and 90 per cent of the National Assembly seats. It owed its dominance primarily to the cattle–owner class, the educated *Tswana* elite, the tribal chiefs and the colonial administration.

The Absence of Significant Socio–Economic Dualisms

Three primary factors account for the absence of dualism in post–Independence Botswana: colonial neglect, the lack of economic development and the retained power of tribal chiefs in internal matters. Because of them, no class or economic interest group delinked from traditional economic activity had emerged at the time of Independence as a source of conflict in building economic and political institutions.

Colonial neglect restricted Botswana's development capacity in the early years of Independence. Colonial rule had neither developed administrative systems nor emphasised revenue–generating activity. Traditional economic structures remained intact, limited largely to subsistence agriculture and cattle ranching. Given the severe shortage of cash–creating work, wage labour became a crucial feature of Botswana's dependence on South Africa; the *Batswana* often migrated to work in the South African mines, although much of the labour was only seasonal. Since the Protectorate had been established primarily to secure trade links between southern and central Africa, colonial rule emphasised only the development of road and rail links through Bechuanaland to South Africa. More positively, colonial interest in Bechuanaland had no origins in rent extraction based on a particular natural resource; this avoided the emergence of dualism in the economic structure and its associated problems.

The most important distributive issue in Botswana concerned cattle ownership, the main source of wealth. Its distribution had become increasingly unequal during the colonial period, to the advantage of the tribal chiefs and Europeans, who thus emerged as more independent and financially dominant over the rest of the economy. At Independence they made up the most powerful economic elite, despite suffering heavy losses due to severe droughts. The cattle–owning class formed the BDP's most powerful constituency and many BDP politicians belonged to it. This class segregation had the potential to generate political dissent, but the Government's policies to accommodate the subsistence needs of the rural population, the majority of the electorate, prevented the rise of significant political opposition.

Absence of Major Ethnic–Based Conflict

Botswana has about 18 tribes, most belonging to the *Tswana* division of the Sotho group of Bantu origin, which came to southern Africa from the north, arriving in Botswana at different times during the 18th and 19th centuries. The *Basarwa* or *San* people (also called Bushmen, *Khoe* or *Khoisan*), on the other hand, are said to be the original inhabitants of the area, from Southwest Africa. As the *Tswana* tribes gained power and wealth in the 19th century, the *San* people, progressively deprived of their property[6], became labourers for the *Tswana* cattlemen and greatly exploited. Eight *Tswana* tribes, accounting for 80 per cent of the *Batswana* population, came to

128

dominate; one of these tribes, the *Ngwato*, 25 per cent of the population, was politically the most powerful. The next largest groups each represent about 10 per cent of the population. The *Ngwato* live in Central District, in the centre–east of Botswana and covering 20 per cent of the total area. The eastern parts of Botswana are the most developed, due both to trade routes and their natural endowments; they also are much more densely populated than the west, where the *Basarwa* live.

The *Basarwa* have traditionally been portrayed as propertyless, leaderless and lawless. Although historians have debated the accuracy of this view, the *Basarwa* have had notably low status since Independence — but not they alone. Most of the population, especially that in remote areas, is landless, and cattle ownership has remained concentrated in the hands of a small *Tswana* elite. Despite this social structure, very low population density impeded the formation of coalitions among either the landless or those not owning cattle against the small minority with access to private wealth. None of the tribes in Botswana either maintained an army or had been involved in any Independence struggle[7]. The lack of any organised channels or means of expressing political opposition has thus reduced the potential for ethnic conflict.

Post–Independence Elements of Political Stability

An able political and economic team has managed Botswana's rapid economic expansion. In essence, the Government adopted a development strategy that primarily targeted market–oriented activity and promoted private entrepreneurship while providing safety nets for the poor. Unlike many other developing countries facing commodity booms, the Government maintained conservative economic policies rather than raising its spending to unsustainable levels, and thus generated economic stability which created a favourable environment for domestic and foreign investment. Political stability has resulted from these favourable economic conditions, a capable administration, a democratic tradition and the establishment of appropriate institutions.

Economic Elements of Political Stability

Rapid expansion of the diamond industry provided a substantial increase in the resources available for economic development. Development spending won the political support of the rural population, allowing the BDP to maintain its majority in all the elections since 1965, albeit with a decreasing share of the vote. Given the vulnerability of the rural population to droughts, safety nets provided by the Government performed a dual function: providing humanitarian assistance to the poor and preventing the emergence of a powerful opposition. The Government used diamond revenues to promote *Batswana* entrepreneurship and improve human and physical capital, which further mobilised political support. Its development strategies and sound economic policies have played a substantial role in creating an economic environment that precluded the formation of special–interest groups and political opposition, despite growing income inequality. Moreover, its managerial capacity has allowed it to secure profitable international agreements, which in turn have facilitated economic and political stability.

Macroeconomic Stability and Economic Growth have provided resources to redistribute to the poor. The discovery of rich diamond mines at the end of 1960s established a growth path unique in Africa. The economy more than doubled in size in real terms (based on 1986 prices) within five years[8]. Between 1966 and 1995, real GDP expanded at 10.7 per cent a year and real per capita GDP at 7.1 per cent. The industrial and agricultural sectors grew at annual average rates of 14.9 per cent and 4.5 per cent (Figure 5.1). Real industrial growth came mainly in mining (24 per cent) and manufacturing (9.7 per cent). Given expectations of high returns, the Government undertook large investments in the mining sector during the 1970s and 1980s. Dramatic structural change has occurred (Figure 5.2); agriculture's share of real GDP plunged from around 40 per cent in the 1960s to about 5 per cent in the 1990s, while mining grew from practically nothing in the late 1960s to more than 40 per cent of GDP in the second half of the 1980s; it accounted for 80 per cent of industrial exports in 1990. This impressive growth and structural change continued unchecked until the 1990s, when the international diamond market suffered a relative downturn.

Figure 5.1 **Output Trends by Sector**
Indices of sectoral output, 1986=100

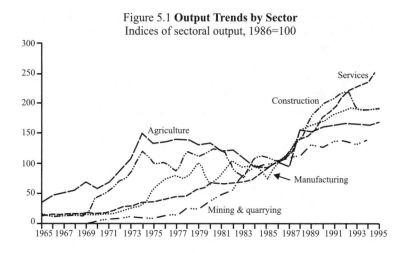

130

Figure 5.2. **Sectoral Shares of GDP**
(Percentage)

While fortuitous exogenous factors have contributed greatly to Botswana's economic achievements, effective economic management has proved equally important for both economic and political stability. When De Beers discovered the diamond mines in 1969, it formed a joint venture with the Government, initially with an 85 per cent share for the company but revised in 1975 to raise the Government's share to 50 per cent. Mining profits have provided the greatest single source of tax revenues, around half of total Government revenues. In 1973, the Government established the Revenue Stabilisation Fund and Public Debt Service Fund to manage the allocation of funds for development. It achieved economic stability with a stable exchange rate, low inflation and positive budget and current account balances[9]. Despite large gains emanating from economic expansion, it cautiously kept the budget in line with the expected long–term flow of revenues and grants in order to maintain a balance not susceptible to short–term fluctuations. Apart from education, fiscal expenditures grew no faster than GDP, and large fiscal surpluses obtained from 1983 onwards (Figures 5.3 and 5.4).

Figure 5.3. **Fiscal Balances**
(Percentage of GDP)

Figure 5.4. **Composition of Fiscal Spending**
(Percentage of GDP)

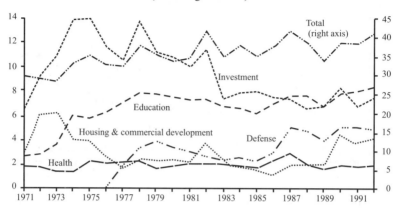

The diamond boom has contributed considerably to balance–of–payments surpluses since 1985, except in 1990 and 1991 after a slowdown in the flow of diamond revenues (Figure 5.5). Foreign direct investment (FDI) inflows, concentrated mainly in mining and the private sector, have also been significant, with the largest share originating from the South Africa–based Anglo–American and De Beers. Such flows depend on good economic performance, political stability, Government incentives and related infrastructure investment. The Government has capably negotiated with foreign investors arrangements considered mutually beneficial for it, the investors, domestic workers and private suppliers. Moreover, Botswana's hard–currency earning capacity relative to other countries in the region (more than 80 per cent of its exports go to the European Community) has made its economy attractive for foreign lending and investment.

Employment has followed the striking developments in output, with total employment rising since the 1970s. Between 1972 and 1990, formal employment increased about five–fold in the Government sector, more than doubling its share of the total active population[10]. Central and local Government has been the single largest employer, although its share in total employment fell to 30 per cent in 1991 from about 40 per cent in 1985. Localisation has taken place at all levels of Government, although much more slowly in professional and technical positions, where expatriates have mostly retained their previous jobs. Employment generation in the Government sector has at times exceeded that in the rest of the economy, but infrastructure spending and social outlays have also generated significant employment in other sectors (Valentine, 1993). The highest employment growth since 1981 has occurred in manufacturing, construction, commerce and finance and business services (Figure 5.6).

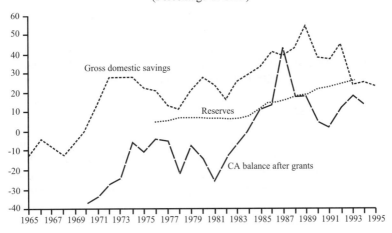

Figure 5.5. **Domestic and Foreign Savings**
(Percentage of GDP)

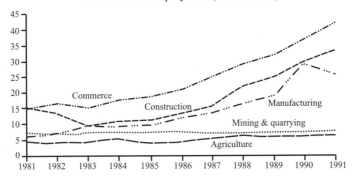

Figure 5.6. **Employment Trends by Sector**
Formal sector employment (in thousands)

Rapid productivity growth in mining has led to a steady decline in the industry's share of national employment since 1975. A capital–intensive operation, diamond mining had peak employment of less than 10 per cent of the formal labour force, and it declined to below 4 per cent by the 1990s. Hence, while formal employment grew over most of the post–Independence period, jobs in mining did not change to any significant degree (Figure 5.6). The industry's main contribution to economic development came through Government revenues rather than job creation; diamond revenues roughly doubled during the 1980s and became the primary source of an annual average increase of about 30 per cent in total Government revenues. Increases in copper, nickel and beef exports also contributed to growing revenues.

Informal–sector employment also grew, although one must infer its magnitude. Between 1966 and 1986, increases in formal employment, about 11 per cent per year, could not absorb all of the additional available work force (Harvey and Lewis, 1990). This provides the basis for an estimate that by 1991 the informal sector's share in the total labour force rose to about 16 per cent, as compared with traditional agriculture's 35 per cent (World Bank, 1993b). Meanwhile, the measured unemployment rate dropped to 16 per cent in 1986 from about 25 per cent just two years earlier; by the early 1990s, it is estimated to have declined further, due to increasing job opportunities in small and medium–scale enterprises.

Employment growth and rapid urbanisation since the 1970s have produced an indirect benefit in increased flows of remittance income to rural households originating in formal employment[11]. Close ties between urban migrants and rural dwellers generated a rising proportion of rural household income from remittances (Valentine, 1993); it grew from 14 per cent in 1975 to 24 per cent in 1985. These domestic remittances per capita have grown with the economy, but permanent labour migration to South Africa has decreased over time.

Development Strategies and Policies. The BDP's development agenda focused on improving the basic social and physical infrastructure. National Development Plans targeted an open economy and a favourable climate for capital flows to achieve growth, social justice, economic independence and sustained development, with a specific emphasis on growth. The Government focused initially on mining investment due to urgent revenue needs. With changes in the economic environment and the political realities accompanying them, however, it modified its development strategy towards the end of the 1960s. In the 1970s, a greater emphasis went on industrialisation as the engine of growth, along with development of the institutional capacity to support it — especially financial, advisory and promotional activities. Further modification came in the 1980s, to give a greater role to the private sector and manufacturing in order to reduce dependence on mining and beef exports.

Unlike many other economies in Africa based on natural resources, prudent fiscal management enabled Botswana to maintain surpluses on its domestic and external accounts despite deterioration in the external terms of trade since the mid–1980s. The incentives leading to the effective management of diamond revenues, rather than to a proliferation of rent–seeking behaviour, have played an important role in the development process. First, the resources that the revenues made available for social spending increased the likelihood that the Government would not face significant opposition. Second, the Government's well–founded expectation of re–election — and thus its long–term horizon and the continuity of administration — have contributed both to a willingness to pursue prudent economic management and to the absence of any widespread abuse of power through rent seeking.

The expectation of long tenure is key. Facilitated by a democratic culture and the lack of powerful, narrow interest groups, it has led the Government to take a strikingly long–term perspective. The expectation of a large share of the gains from a growing economy over a long period provided the incentive to promote an efficient economic system. Even though the Government may not have represented the whole of the society, this expectation still provided an incentive, first to reinvest — rather than spend on luxury–good imports, for example — and second to redistribute, in order to reduce the potential for political instability. This has been Botswana's development strategy, reinforced by the interests of the primary mining enterprise, De Beers, in maintaining a sound economy to promote greater efficiency in diamond mining.

The Government also has emphasised development of basic infrastructure, such as health, education, transport and market facilities. Despite very limited domestic resources initially, it had achieved great success by the 1980s in improving the infrastructure and providing people with relatively equal access to it[12]. Although the state deployed significant resources to this end, however, rural areas did not receive much employment–generating, productive investment. This has been the major criticism of the development strategy.

The Government's agricultural strategy gave heavy emphasis to the development of commercial cattle ranching in the early development plans, as a result of its close ties with the commercial cattle owners. Grazing land covered only about 20 per cent of the total land area due to water scarcity, yet beef accounted for 80 per cent of agricultural output — and beef exports for about 40 per cent of export revenues in the 1970s. The Tribal Grazing Land Policy (TGLP), formulated in the early 1970s along with other land–allocation policies to facilitate the development of commercial cattle farming, stimulated a rapid spread of commercial ranches. This aggravated landlessness among subsistence farmers and led to even more unequal cattle ownership; in 1975, 45 per cent of the rural population owned no cattle (Tordoff, 1988), and by 1991, 74 per cent did not (Good, 1994). In the early 1980s, the Presidential Commission on Employment Opportunities revealed that only a third of development spending had gone to rural areas, where most of the population lived.

Provoked partly by reduced rural support in the 1969 elections, the Government started to give more attention to rural development in the 1970s. In 1973, the Accelerated Rural Development Programme focused on rural physical infrastructure, but did nothing to improve agricultural production. Rural infrastructure development and the involvement of local administrations in the implementation of smaller development projects were used by the Government, however, to mobilise political support. In the 1980s, national development plans began to focus specifically on improving agricultural production.

Droughts inevitably interrupted development. The Government sought to mitigate their impact through measures under the Drought Relief Programme (DRP), initiated in 1982 and intended to provide safety nets against droughts as well as promote agricultural development through asset management and maintenance. During the Fifth National Development Plan (1980–85), the Arable Land Development Programme (ALDEP) provided only small–scale farmers with credit, inputs and subsidies. Commercial loans, the largest source of agricultural credit, went mostly to large–scale farmers owning cattle herds. The Sixth Plan (1986–91) directed more resources to the agricultural sector and included medium–scale farmers, through the Accelerated Rainfed Arable Programme (ARAP). This programme provided subsidised inputs and cash grants to enlarge arable lands. It failed because subsistence farming methods did not change, and only a small number of already wealthy farmers benefited. Programmes to modernise remote–area farming also did not succeed, as Government subsidies served only as drought relief[13]. Nonetheless, the DRP mobilised significant rural political support by providing much–needed subsidies to overcome deteriorated living conditions during drought years. Its contribution was substantial; it supported about half of agricultural GDP during the drought years (1982–87), benefiting about 60 per cent of the rural population (Valentine, 1993).

Following the significant build–up in diamond revenues in the 1970s, the BDP in the 1980s emphasised private–sector development in industrialisation. It provided infrastructure investment, such as transport and communication, and in 1982 created several incentive and promotion schemes for the private sector. Although one can debate whether these schemes contributed much to economic diversification and employment generation, it is generally accepted that they enhanced political support and the development of small–scale entrepreneurs in 1985–90 (Danevad, 1995)[14].

Income Distribution and Wages Policy. Botswana has fairly marked income inequality between rural and urban dwellers and within the rural sector; urban incomes are only relatively more equally distributed. Recent statistics indicate that 55 per cent of the rural population and 40 per cent of the urban one live in absolute poverty. The TGLP contributed heavily to increasing inequality in rural areas; under it cattle owners could obtain more land — as well as finance and infrastructure — despite decreasing land available for subsistence farmers, especially the *Basarwa*. Moreover, as formal–sector urban wages increased, rural dwellers' access to formal employment remained very limited. Significant Government aid to offset the negative effects of droughts has not sufficed to maintain the living standards of off–drought periods. Droughts and rural policy together have pushed down the real incomes of the poorest households in both relative and absolute terms. The incomes of the poorest 40 per cent of the population (urban and rural) fell by 27 per cent between 1972 and 1986 (Harvey and Lewis, 1990), and stood at just over 11 per cent of total income in 1994. Thus, both the urban poor and the *Basarwa* became part of a nascent opposition constituency.

The BDP Government first introduced an incomes policy in 1972, to prevent the extreme inequalities that could have resulted from increased demand for scarce skilled labour and management as the diamond industry boomed. It consciously aimed to reduce wage gaps between urban and rural areas and within the state sector. The private sector has seen similar initiatives, but since the 1980s, it has become more difficult to control expanding wages there, especially in branches benefiting from growing diamond revenues. This has led to widening differentials between the public and private sectors and consequent public–sector pressure to increase wages. In 1990, the Government started to adopt a relatively more liberal wage policy, paving the way for collective bargaining (Danevad, 1995). This policy change accorded with the general strategy favouring market mechanisms and reduced state intervention, but it also led to an 18.7 per cent increase in the central Government wage bill, mostly for middle and senior management. Blue–collar public workers then demanded a 15.4 per cent increase in 1991. The Government rejected these demands, which widened wage differentials between the private and the public sectors, but at least signalled a desire for smaller private wage increases than before. Wages of foreign workers were already subject to lesser control, and the gap between expatriate and local employees persisted or increased, although skill differentials usually justified it.

Incomes policy did generally succeed in reducing income gaps by increasing the lowest incomes. The minimum wage increased by 26 per cent in 1980. In the civil service, the ratio of highest to lowest incomes improved from 36:1 in 1966 to 16:1 in 1987 (Meisender, 1994), although the ratio of top public–service salaries to the minimum wage reached 38:1 in 1992 (Good, 1994). Despite the real wage increases, unemployment fell sharply. Three critical problems remain: the large state sector, relatively high unemployment and high wages in relation to productivity.

Regional Policies. At Independence, half the Government budget depended on British aid which had tried since the late 1950s to make up for long–neglected infrastructure investment. The economy offered few opportunities for taxation; levies on cattle ranching presented an obvious but unrealistic option because the political elite and the cattle–owning class largely coincided. Given the relatively large import component of the economy, customs revenues appeared as the most appropriate source. In 1969, the terms of the South Africa Customs Union Agreement (SACU) with Lesotho, Swaziland and South Africa were renegotiated, increasing Botswana's economic ties with the Union countries and leading to a drastic increase in the share of customs duties in total Government revenues, from one–fifth in 1969 to half in 1970[15]. The SACU benefited Botswana as it enabled it to increase its access to transportation, infrastructure and manufactured goods from South Africa, free of restrictions. The expansion of the mining industry in subsequent years led to a further increase in fiscal revenues from imports of essential capital goods[16].

Botswana also made diplomatic efforts to gain the attention of the donor community by reducing its dependence on South Africa and through its active membership in the SADC, which also targeted reduced economic dependence on South Africa. The country was able to obtain Scandinavian aid due to its relatively democratic and uncorrupted regime and its lack of involvement in the political turmoil of southern Africa. In 1975, after the United Kingdom joined the EC, Botswana gained access to EC preferences and benefited from the Generalised System of Preferences. The diversification of exports from beef, mainly directed to South African markets, towards copper, nickel and diamonds, mostly bound for Europe and the United States, also significantly changed Botswana's direction of trade. In 1989, 80 per cent of exports went to markets outside Africa, which reduced dependence on South Africa in transport and communications as well as for export markets. Yet import dependence on South Africa did not drop; in 1993, 82 per cent of imports still came from SACU countries, among which South Africa had the largest share.

Botswana's relatively moderate relationships with South Africa and Rhodesia, despite its ideological opposition to their racial politics, arose mainly from commercial relations. Its small economy did not permit self–sufficiency, and dependence on the South African trade and labour markets was too vital to be broken. Besides the trade linkages, South Africa also provided a major source of employment, seasonally and in times of drought. South Africa itself has had long–term economic interests in Botswana, such as its large investments in mining. Moreover, the absence of confrontation between whites and Africans, even during the colonial period, and the absence of a permanent guerrilla base in Botswana gave less reason to South Africa to play a destabilising role there than in other front–line states.

Institutional Elements of Political Stability

Botswana inherited no well–developed administration, no dual economic structure and no strong interest–group organisations at Independence. Leaving aside exogenous good fortune, the managerial ability and institution building of the post–Independence Government largely account for the subsequent course of political development and for how interest–group organisations evolved. Political stability in Botswana has had five important determinants: the non–ethnic approach of the Government; consensus building and a reconciliatory approach in administration that built on traditional democratic elements; the nature of interest groups; development of a political opposition; and the lack of widespread corruption.

Ethnicity. Even though no segregation policy existed, the *Basarwa* remained disadvantaged along with others in remote areas. Despite these great inequalities, the Government managed to mobilise rural support and averted the development of a rural opposition, helped by cultural and structural factors not conducive to effective organisation of rural people. That most development took place in non–traditional sectors and outside areas that could be identified with specific ethnic populations helped create the perception of an ethnically neutral policy stance. That mining employment, unlike mining production, did not explode, strictly limited the emergence of any dualism and avoided major distortion in employment opportunities across ethnic regions. Most indigenous entrepreneurial activity, which the Government encouraged, took place in the urban areas.

The state tried consciously to de–emphasise ethnic politics, particularly by appointing elite members of non–*Tswana* groups to Government positions. The two main political parties, BDP and BNF, have enjoyed multi–ethnic support, and the universal approach to politics by their leaders after Independence entailed campaigning all across the country and avoiding political appointments based on ethnicity. The presidential power transition in 1980 illustrates the insignificance of ethnic segmentation in Botswana. Following the death of Seretse Khama, Quett Masire, the former Vice President, was chosen as the new President, even though he belonged to a much less powerful tribe, the *Bangwaketse*. Still more surprising, his tribe had traditionally supported the BNF.

Thus, ethnicity has formed a base neither for policies of discrimination and segregation, nor for the concentration of power or prestige. The BDP Government has been quite conservative in its attitudes towards ethnicity and has not been sympathetic to narrower ethnic interests. In general, it has discounted ethnic variation within the political process of consensus building. That the non–*Tswana* also recognise the need to be part of a homogeneous society has subdued prospects that opposition parties could mobilise political support on ethnic bases.

Administrative Policies. Botswana has a strong central state and a decentralised administrative system that ensures — although in part only ceremonially — a high level of political participation. The representative electoral system, as opposed to a proportional system, favours strong Government and allocates little room for minority–party representation. Decision making takes place mainly at the centre, but people can participate informally in the approval, or disapproval, and implementation of almost every project at the local level. Disapproval of projects at this level is tantamount to an informal veto, which usually triggers negotiations between traditional leaders and the Government until a consensus emerges[17]. Thus, although local representatives, including the traditional leaders, do not participate in initial decision making, the process makes public policy more transparent and the system reasonably democratic. In addition to the influence of economic stability and the political mobilisation of the rural sector through redistributive policies, the Government has maintained political stability through use of this participatory style of administration.

Botswana changed its constitution after the 1969 elections when Seretse Khama reassumed his post as President, to give the Government the form of a "parliamentary republic", a synthesis of the presidential and parliamentary systems. It gives a relatively powerful role to the executive along with a significant one for the President in it, with a combined executive and legislative body (Danevad, 1993). Within this system, the Ministry of Finance and Development Planning (MFDP) has an especially important position, although inter–ministerial bargaining decides the allocation of funds. Parliament has the power to influence decisions, but the executive has the final word (Danevad, 1993). The coherence of economic policies and the strength of the centre are further enhanced by a small Parliament of 40 members that makes negotiation and consensus building relatively easy.

An important political issue in the early years of Independence involved redefining the role of the tribal chiefs within the newly established democratic institutions. The Government legislated a series of reforms that limited their executive power and a major part of their legislative power. At the same time, the new organisation of rural administration institutionalised a place for them, giving the House of Chiefs an advisory capacity at the level of local administration. This role has remained mostly ceremonial.

Decentralisation of administration received an early emphasis. While old institutions were maintained to some extent, many of the tribal chiefs' traditional roles were allocated to the organs of the Government. The Local Government Act of 1965 established the District Councils (DCs) that took over many of the chiefs' administrative and development responsibilities in health, education and infrastructure. The DCs were run by both locally elected and centrally nominated councillors, and constituted half of local Government employees. The Customary Courts Acts of 1966 and 1986 limited the judicial power of the chiefs and *kgotlas*. An independent judiciary, handled by the Tribal Administration, was maintained to enhance the democratic nature of the state, although an organisation of the district administration supervised it. Within this system, citizens were left free to choose between the common and the customary courts in simple cases; many trials were still held in the customary courts. Following the Tribal Land Act of 1968, the District Land Boards (LBs) gradually took over responsibility for land allocation, further limiting the political and economic power of the chiefs — although the chiefs and their representatives were appointed to the LBs along with representatives of the Government[18]. The Local Government Act placed tax collection in the hands of elected authorities; this not only further reduced the traditional chiefs' power but also deprived them of a key opportunity to accumulate wealth.

As a further element in decentralisation, District Development Commissions (DDCs) were established in 1970 as non–political advisory bodies made up of public–sector representatives, to play an important role in preparing District Development Plans (DDPs). DDPs have rarely found their way into the National Development Plan, however, due to lack of district capacity to prepare them and a lack of co–ordination with the National Plan. These inefficiencies have caused National Plans often to neglect district resource–allocation priorities.

The centre has exercised control over local administrations through two main channels: first, the DCs, generally lacking resources of their own, have relied on central Government transfers; second, loyalty to the Government has been an important criterion in the selection of administrative staff. Some chiefs strongly opposed the establishment of DCs as restricting their traditional power. Chief Bathoen of the *Ngwaketse* resigned from his traditional post over this issue and became the leader of the opposition BNF, which provides an example of how traditional political leadership was transformed. Eventually, the conflict between the chiefs and the Government became marginalised as one between the older, less educated generation and a growing educated elite that supported the BDP and its democratic institutions. The chiefs' assimilation into the new order went far to control potential conflict between the traditional and modern structures.

As this assimilation demonstrates, seeking consensus has been an important element of decision making. Government ministers have usually explained policy proposals through *kgotlas* before reaching Cabinet decisions. While the *kgotla* institution itself may not be fully democratic — it excludes women and minority groups from local debates — holding public debates and national conferences before *kgotlas* prior to implementing any major development project or economic initiative (except for mining and roads) does indicate a will to use democratic mechanisms. Moreover, while public policy plans, targets and decisions generally are determined centrally, they typically are made explicit and thus open to monitoring[19]. Public influence is limited to implementation of national policies, however, and does not extend to broader participation in decision making. Nonetheless, such public participation, although partly ceremonial, did facilitate the emergence of a stable political environment.

While the authority of the traditional chiefs progressively waned, the traditional institutional structures quite successfully amalgamated with the emerging ones. The role of Europeans in the state bureaucracy and policy design was maintained, while localisation took place only slowly. The institutional features that have contributed to political stability are themselves the product of the *Batswana* culture and its stability. The absence of hierarchies or ranks across the tribal or ethnic groupings, traditional democratic culture and the small size of the Parliament helped in building a consensus around the national development objectives. Along with favourable economic shocks, this consensus–building attribute of the state and society has facilitated the enhancement and maintenance of functioning societal and political institutions that carry forward elements of the traditional structures.

Interest Group Formation. Economic development and the emergence of dominant interest groups relate dynamically to the evolution of political interests. Botswana inherited very little interest–group organisation. It had not even had a strong agricultural lobby because the political elite itself largely represented the interests of cattle owners. This absence of interest groups persisted until at least the 1980s, due in part to a lack of experience, organisational power and incentives and in part, certainly, to a negative official attitude. Committee members of trade unions were not allowed to hold the positions as full–time jobs. The Labour Relations Law of 1983 limited union freedom to organise and negotiate. Labour unrest was generally declared illegal. As the private press began to expand from the late 1980s, some newspapers received Government threats of legal action and some foreign journalists were expelled. The media initiated a form of self–censorship and in general remained a weak organ of civil society. More recently, a general trend towards more visible and relatively more political interest groups has emerged, as reflected in industrial actions, union strikes and the private press[20]. It has not reached a level posing any serious challenge to the Government.

NGOs, mostly donor–funded, played a relatively important role in developing the basic social infrastructure until the 1970s, when increasing mining revenues enabled the Government to step in more actively. As they lost prominence in this changing environment, and despite official discouragement, many important domestic interest groups emerged. The Farmers' Association lobbied for commercial farmers and livestock owners, usually at the expense of subsistence farmers and traditional landholders. The Botswana Confederation of Commerce, Industry and Manpower (BOCCIM) lobbied for tax and price liberalisation and market incentives — although the interests of its small members often conflicted with those of its larger ones. About 20 trade unions, gathered under the umbrella of the Botswana Federation of Trade Unions (BFTU), represented some 10 per cent of the labour force (twice that in the private sector). Although not especially powerful, the BFTU managed to play an instrumental role in the abolition of wage controls and restrictions on trade–union activities in the 1990s. The Botswana Mining Workers Union was strong, however, although it had no major political power base because mining employment accounted for such a small part of the total. Civil–service workers and secondary–school teachers also had unions; the civil service was the relatively better organised. The Employers Federation showed a powerful ability to access the Government and its resources.

Such groups were shunned by the Government and thus had relatively limited representation in formal decision making. Even politicians outside the Cabinet appear to have had only limited influence on policy, and only through informal channels. The advisory process for incomes policies illustrated the dominance of the political elite; although representatives of trade unions, private bodies and parastatals participated in the forums, decisions typically were heavily biased towards the Government interest. Strikes in the 1990s against increasing wage inequalities reflected discontent with the prevailing decision–making process. The Government responded to these shows of dissent by declaring strikes illegal. More recently, however, private–sector interests appear to have gained a larger influence over incomes–policy decisions. This reflects in part the emergence of a *Tswana* entrepreneurial class, including retired and current Government officials; their share–holding in private companies gives them a relatively clear group definition, with interests mostly in urban activities such as commerce, real estate and manufacturing.

Political Opposition and Electoral Politics. After the 1965 elections, three opposition parties emerged: the Botswana National Front (BNF), the Botswana People's Party (BPP) and the Botswana Independence Party (BIP). BNF, the main opposition, has its constituency mainly among economically vulnerable social groups and those who favour traditional authority, in contrast with the BDP which at times has perceived the tribal authorities as a potential source of instability. The BNF favours nationalisation, protection of real incomes and increased trade–union freedom, so it has attracted workers and the unemployed. Its economic policy agenda for minerals, natural resources and diversification has not differed much from that of the BDP. Its share of the vote has increased sharply since the 1980s (Table 5.1), although it generally has not presented a well–defined political alternative or challenge to Government economic policies.

Table 5.1. **Election Results since Independence**

| Election year | Electoral participation (%) | Share (%) of | |
		BDP	BNF
1965	74	80	-
1969	55	68	14
1974	31	77	12
1979	58	75	13
1984	77	68	21
1989	68	65	27
1994	-	55	37

The long–term erosion of support for the BDP has reflected the growing discontent of the traditional chiefs with reforms that limit their authority. The party's temporary recovery from the trend in the 1974 elections stemmed in part from pre–election increases in local Government and civil–service employment and wages. Although political competition has increased over time, the BDP has retained its strength in Parliament, helped by the "representative–majority" electoral system which favours a strong Government over weak coalitions. The increasing power of BNF opposition has clearly had an impact on the BDP's policy agenda. For example, BNF pressure in favour of free primary and secondary education in 1988 won BDP agreement shortly before the elections in 1989. Generation–gap influences have begun to affect politics as much as interest–group formation. Younger groups in the Government favour market–oriented policies more than cattle–owner interests, and younger members of the trade unions prefer the BNF while older, more traditional union members continue their loyalty to the BDP.

Avenues for Corruption. Several socio–economic and political factors have hindered widespread corrupt practices. First, official emphasis on a growth strategy oriented to the private sector has limited state interference in the productive sectors of the economy. Free access of bureaucrats and politicians to personal wealth through private ownership[21] has reduced incentives for rent seeking in the state sector, although it may have led to favouritism in the allocation of funds to the private sector. Generally, formal criteria and strict rules about the allocation of funds, managed by a narrow political and bureaucratic elite, have tended to discourage corruption. Second, the Government, with its notably long political horizon, could afford to allocate resources to long–term development projects rather than to short–term ventures geared to rent extraction. Moreover, politicians normally engaged in private commercial activities, such as cattle ranching, which deflected them from abusing their political positions to generate income. Indeed, they typically approached policy making from a strongly technical perspective. Third, continuity in governmental appointments and the slow rate of localisation contributed to quality in administration. The technocratic approach emphasised institutional development and market mechanisms, which reduced the potential for rent–seeking behaviour.

Nevertheless, abuses of loan funds and malpractices in land sales and housing surfaced in the 1990s. One issue arose because parastatal boards included members from related ministries, increasing the likelihood of malpractice in the distribution of public resources. In 1991, the National Development Bank (NDB), established primarily for agriculture and development financing, and the Small Borrowers Fund that it managed for the Government collapsed under accumulated arrears as a result of lending to uncreditworthy borrowers — and despite several debt reschedulings and write–offs by the Government in the 1980s. Although some of the debtors included high–ranking Government officials, including ministers, no resignations followed after these revelations. Other public lending institutions, such as the Agricultural Marketing Board and the Botswana Co–operative Bank, also have incurred sizeable losses. Further incidents involved the Vice President, the Minister for Local Government and the Minister for Agriculture, who claimed their innocence and continued to hold their Governmental positions. The incentive schemes for private–sector development also came under suspicion as creating an environment for fraud and corruption because they were not entirely transparent and provided funds on a discretionary, case–by–case basis.

Such incidents provoked citizen and student demonstrations, which stimulated the Government to launch extensive inquiries that resulted in convictions and dismissals of involved officials. Provoked by the scandals, signs of division within the ruling party emerged as regional and generational rivalries started to surface. On balance, however, corruption in the bureaucracy has not been viewed as widespread or systemic and seems to be restricted to a small group. The Government has shown seriousness about taking measures in response to it; in 1994, it established the Directorate on Corruption and Economic Crime to examine public bodies to facilitate the discovery of corruption, analyse practices conducive to corruption, investigate cases of corruption and offences against the fiscal laws, and assist other law enforcement agencies also investigating cases of the misuse of public revenues. It also advises, trains and enlists public support against corruption (Hope, 1995).

Potential Sources of Political Instability

The combination of a democratic culture, good governance and favourable exogenous factors has brought three decades of political stability to Botswana. Economic management and the institutional structures have conformed closely to society's cultural and developmental needs since Independence. Although many of the structural elements of political stability — managerial capacity, the democratic and moderate political tradition and market–oriented institutions — should continue to benefit Botswana in the long run, exogenous events are necessarily less reliable. Moreover, several development problems could threaten future political stability. Factors such as rapid urbanisation, insufficient agricultural development and economic diversification, if accompanied by worsening economic conditions, could lead to empowerment of the political opposition and possible tensions. The economic growth potential will thus greatly affect Botswana's political prospects.

Current diamond reserves will last for a long time, and the monopolistic nature of the diamond markets should protect diamond revenues against the international price fluctuations typical of classic commodities markets. Yet both diamond sales and cattle exports, the two main sources of revenue in Botswana, are to a considerable degree externally controlled — by the De Beers Central Selling Organisation and by the EU — while domestic infrastructure spending and major services to the population remain mainly centred around them. This vulnerability revealed itself in 1992, for example, when De Beers reduced delivery entitlements of all diamond producers by 25 per cent in reaction to the increased supply of rough diamonds smuggled from Angola[22]. International market vulnerability and Botswana's limited discretion in supply decisions for its key exports point to the need for economic diversification. Communications, construction and manufacturing account only for about 10 per cent of GDP, and one cannot reasonably view agriculture as having enough growth potential to pull the economy forward. Instead, given Botswana's small markets and land–locked position, the service sector appears to have the greatest potential for future economic growth. Exploiting it will require investment in human technical capacity and financial services.

With sound internal and external accounts, Botswana has attracted foreign investment and retained a significant share of the internally generated commercial gains. Foreign debt, although it increased during the 1980s, remains sustainable, and foreign exchange reserves could finance more than two years of imports[23]. Yet dependence on South Africa for imports as well as foreign investment constitutes a potential problem for future stability. The potential effects on Botswana's foreign trade relations of the reforms in South Africa and Zimbabwe remain unclear. Although liberalisation policies in the region could be beneficial in many ways, the net effect on the current account may not be positive, given Botswana's relatively low productivity and high wages. In the short run, the Zimbabwe reforms may have negative effects on Botswana's trade, as occurred with the devaluation of the Zimbabwe dollar in 1993. Given its stable currency and large foreign reserves, however, Botswana could gain from a comparative advantage in tourism and, especially, financial services.

Prior to 1991, interest rates, largely fixed by the Bank of Botswana (BOB), were negative in real terms, providing incentives to borrow at the expense of the lending institutions. Since then, financial reforms have led to an emphasis on indirect policy instruments and positive real interest rates. Although this initially affected private investors adversely, positive interest rates and measures such as the introduction of BOB certificates and revised liquid asset ratios represent reforms important for the long–term stability of the financial system, and should contribute to overall economic stability.

The interest organisations formed by the market–oriented *Tswana* bourgeoisie have grown, especially in urban areas, since the 1980s. In view of their weak representation in the Government, they have associated themselves with the three opposition parties (the BNF, BPP and BIP). Meanwhile, based on the support of minority ethnic groups (mostly non–*Tswana*), these three parties considered forming an electoral coalition to unite the opposition to the BDP. In 1991, they formalised the process under the name of the People's Progressive Front, but it ended abruptly in 1994 following the death of one of its main promoters. If such coalitions were to thrust ethnic issues deeply into politics, a potential danger to stability could arise (Holm and Molutsi, 1992).

Nevertheless, the organisation of such groups has so far remained weak and posed no danger. Reflecting discontent with widening income inequalities and lack of participation in the Government, BNF has won an increasing number of votes from Government employees, urban and non–*Tswana* groups and traditionalists since the 1970s. This support seems to reflect increasing inequalities within the urban and rural sectors, rather than a response to a poorly defined alternative policy agenda. In time, the opposition could develop better organisation and gain enough power to challenge the Government. In such circumstances, and given the likelihood of increasing political competition and shorter political tenure, establishing and developing essential market institutions becomes crucial in maintaining incentives to pursue good economic policies for sustainable development.

Notes

1. *Batswana* refers to the people of Botswana. *Motswana* is one person and *Setswana* the language. *Tswana*, the root word, represents the cultural attributes of about 80 per cent of the population, made up of eight principal ethnic sub–groups.

2. *Kgotla* is a traditional institution in Botswana, where the tribal chief listens to the voice of the tribal assembly on community matters. It consists of all the tribe (excluding those under 30 years of age) although women can only attend, but not speak. The tribal chief represents the final authority. A concentric social structure rather than hierarchical rule dominates the tribal tradition, however, and the *kgotla* can outvote the chief. The traditional administration thus has a somewhat democratic cast.

3. The effect of droughts is much less severe on cattle breeders and those who can find seasonal employment in South Africa than on subsistence farmers.

4. The poll taxes also skewed cattle ownership. People with only a few cattle faced increasing pressure to sell them to finance tax payments, part of which went to the chiefs as commission.

5. Seretse Khama's marriage to a European in 1948 received wide criticism from the tribal community, the British and the white regimes in southern Africa, but it later came to symbolise his non–racial stance.

6. The *Tswana* elite emerged as only a small proportion of the rural population but owned most of the only form of private wealth, cattle, and prohibited their workers, mostly *Basarwa*, from owning cattle on their lands.

7. In fact, Botswana did not decide until 1977 to establish its own small army in the face of Rhodesian border crossings in pursuit of guerrillas, even though Botswana did not provide permanent bases for guerrillas.

8. The opening of a copper–nickel complex also contributed to the expansion of the mining sector.

9.   By leaving the Rand Monetary Area in 1976, Botswana gained independence in the formulation of its monetary policies.

10. During 1982–91, annual average employment growth was 7.9 per cent in the public sector and 9.9 per cent in the private and parastatal sectors combined (World Bank, 1993*b*).

11. About 30 per cent of the population was classified as urban by 1995, as opposed to about 10 per cent in 1970 (World Bank, 1995*c*).

12. The illiteracy rate fell from about 80 per cent at Independence to less than 30 per cent by the 1990s, and the child mortality rate is now one of the lowest among developing countries.

13. Infrastructure spending also aimed to improve the facilities for the distribution of grains. The Botswana Agricultural Marketing Board (BAMB) was established for this purpose, but agricultural pricing policies mostly favoured large producers who could sell their surplus to BAMB at subsidised prices.

14. Initiatives included the Financial Assistance Policy (FAP) of 1982, mainly geared to generating employment opportunities and channelling local entrepreneurs to industrial activities; and the Trade and Industrial Promotion Agency (TIPA) and the Industrial Development Policy (IDP) of 1984, directing industrialisation strategy to the enhancement of employment opportunities, the provision of incentives for the *Batswana*, and achieving a better spatial distribution of income–earning opportunities.

15. It fell thereafter due to the increased relative share of mineral exports. The revenues did grow in real terms.

16. As of 1992, customs revenues remain the second largest source of revenue for the Government (24 per cent of total revenues). Smaller countries in the Union, including Botswana, suffered, however, from revenue collection lags, for which South Africa was mainly responsible, and from the concentration of industry in South Africa. Despite attempts to improve these conditions, the SACU remained throughout 1980s under the renegotiated terms of 1969.

17. Disagreements with Government policy proposals at the local level have in some instances led to prolonged debates until a compromise is finally reached; this is illustrated in the case of a programme to enable the private use of the tribal communal lands and wildlife management, where the debate lasted for 15 years.

18. Both the Village Development Committees, established with the same act, and the LBs were linked to the DCs.

19. Except for decisions regarding defence spending.

20. Until the 1980s, the only daily newspaper in Botswana was Government–owned. Private newspapers started up in the 1980s without major censorship, although some Government interference exists, as evidenced by the expulsion of some foreign journalists following their coverage of the strikes in 1991.

21. The Botswana elite could engage in agriculture and land development activities and (as of 1982) hold minority shares in private companies.

22. But note that this monopolistic tactic held prices up, and the Government's prudent, long–term management practices allowed it to weather the short–term drop in diamond revenues relatively easily.

23. Many large projects have been financed through foreign borrowing, and imports still constitute more than half of the national income.

Chapter 6

Determinants of Political Stability in Malawi: 1964–96

Introduction

Nyasaland — now Malawi — became a British Protectorate in 1891, and part of the Federation of Rhodesia and Nyasaland between 1953 and 1963. Its uneasy role in that Federation had much bearing on later political developments in Malawi itself. A non–violent nationalist movement, the Nyasaland African Congress (NAC), which dated its origin to 1944, opposed the Federation unsuccessfully and could not prevent its formation in 1953. It did not retreat, however, and in fact intensified its opposition towards the end of 1950s, when activists invited Dr. H. Kamuzu Banda to return from a self–imposed exile of about 40 years as a unifying figure to lead the NAC. Dr. Banda was a well–known, charismatic figure, highly respected for his achievements in exile. After the NAC was banned in 1959, he became leader of the Malawi Congress Party (MCP), formed by an active opponent of the Federation, Orton Chirwa. An unarmed nationalist struggle led to the dissolution of the Federation in 1963 and to Independence in 1964.

That Nyasaland did not attract as many European settlers and as much investment as the rest of the Federation relates closely to Malawi's development potential after Independence[1]. In 1964, it was one of the poorest countries in the world[2]. Increased investment flows after World War II had induced considerable economic growth between 1953 and 1963, but they remained insufficient to alter Malawi's status greatly. Thereafter, and despite the country's poor physical and human infrastructure at Independence and its limited natural resources, its economic performance until the late 1970s was generally regarded as impressive; in the 1970s, the economy grew on average twice as fast as the rest of sub–Saharan Africa. Favourable exogenous economic conditions and a relatively uncorrupted public sector influenced this performance. Private business was encouraged, although estate development, considered the engine

151

of growth, and industrial licensing remained largely linked with political loyalties. Malawi was the only western–aligned country in the region, except for South Africa, which helped its international trade relations.

Starting in the late 1970s, a series of exogenous shocks distorted economic performance. Agricultural output fell due to droughts in 1980 and 1981, the terms of trade fell drastically following the two oil shocks, export demand declined and transport costs increased due to the war in Mozambique. The resulting increase in foreign borrowing and in interest rates led to a higher debt burden and to reduced investment (Annexes 1 and 2 report the main macroeconomic indicators for 1970–95). The external shocks revealed the economy's weaknesses: heavy dependence on agriculture and primary–commodity exports. The lack of economic diversification and the MCP's dominant role in both the state and private sectors, coupled with severe political repression, prevented the organisation of interest groups and an effective political opposition until the 1990s. Thus, Malawi achieved only an apparent political stability, mainly *via* the mechanisms of state and political control, rather than a real absence of potential political opposition.

Concentrated political and economic structures largely worked as mechanisms of political control and led to increasing inequality and poverty. The economic downturn that started in the late 1970s aggravated these trends and greatly contributed to the escalation of political opposition to one–party rule. The threat to stability manifested itself in widespread international and domestic disapproval of the regime's non–democratic machinery. By the early 1990s, political opposition had started to be voiced by leaders in exile, the donor community and the church, which was especially instrumental in invoking a movement towards democracy. Widespread strikes, demonstrations and riots by urban and rural workers, students and civil workers led to a democratic transition in 1994, without much resistance from the MCP or its overzealous paramilitary force, the Malawi Young Pioneers (MYP).

Fundamental Elements of Political Stability

The British colonial administration had a monopoly on estate ownership and Europeans owned the roughly 2 per cent of the area that contained the best arable land. It did not invest much, and no significantly rich natural resource could be used to generate rents. It largely neglected social services and education, leaving them to the Christian missionaries, who influenced much of the population through formal education and religious teachings. By reducing the significance of ethnic differentials, the church gradually became a unifying force among the Africans. The lack of major ethnic rivalries facilitated unified action against the Federation with Rhodesia. With his massive popularity, Dr. Banda became the unifying figure of the independence movement; his speeches invoked civil disorder throughout the country, demanding an end to the Federation and resulting in Independence.

Malawi has a very diversified ethnic population, mostly scattered across the country. No major group has a military or numerical dominance. At Independence, the African population was relatively homogeneous in terms of its socio–economic characteristics. The absence of major ethnic divisions, a dearth of inherited socio–economic interest groups due to the economic structure and policies of the colonial period, and the poor education base facilitated the imposition of political control by the post–Independence government and permitted the appearance of political stability which lasted about three decades.

Absence of Major Ethnic Divisions

Most of the seven major ethnic groups have Bantu origins. The largest, the *Chewa*, comprises 28.3 per cent of the population, followed by the *Nyanja* (15.3 per cent), *Lomwe* (11.8 per cent) and *Yao* (11.2 per cent)[3]. Inter–ethnic marriages and trade are common, indicating no significant ethnic rivalries. The numerical and regional distribution of the major ethnic groups implies only small potential for the emergence of ethnic–based power centres. The *Chewa* (Dr. Banda's group) is the most concentrated, in the Central Region; the *Nyanja* dominate the Southern Region but also are scattered over the rest of the country, while the *Yao* also concentrate in the Southern Region. All others are dispersed widely across the country. The Northern Region has many ethnic groups, including the *Ngoni* who, like the *Yao*, historically had relatively greater military and political power and, unlike them, practised an indirect but hierarchical rule that allowed traditional chiefs to govern according to customary law.

The Nyasaland Protectorate established new districts administered by European tax collectors. Traditional chiefs became assimilated into the colonial legal and administrative systems, in which their power and prestige eroded substantially and their informal authority was limited to the trials of Africans only. As the region remained generally at peace, this reduced the possibility of ethnic–based organisation[4]. Moreover, because colonial rule imposed high taxes on Africans, many Africans had to migrate to neighbouring countries in search of wage employment. This not only weakened ethnic links but also increased the sentiments for African unity that facilitated the national struggle for Independence[5].

Native Associations, the first political organisations, started to emerge in 1912. They sought improvement of local conditions and contributed to the creation of regional rather than ethnic identities due to the diverse ethnic affiliations of their members. The post–Independence government further emphasised national unity by pursuing policies to prevent ethnic–based political divisions. In 1968 the most common language, *Chichewa*, understood by three–quarters of the population and spoken by the two largest ethnic groups that constitute about half of it, was declared the national language, beside English. Ethnic rivalries remained virtually absent in the Cabinet and the police, which reflected a generally balanced composition of members from different ethnic groups[6]. Political divisions that surfaced in the 1990s generally reflected regional, not ethnic identities. The breakdown of votes in the 1994 elections clearly revealed this for all three main parties.

The influence of Christian missionaries also contributed to the lack of ethnically affiliated power centres. The spread of Christianity had a unifying effect on Africans, evident in the emergence during the 1920s and 1930s of many independent African churches which emphasised improvement of the socio–economic conditions of Africans. The church had important effects on Malawi society, both as a unifying element in the independence movement, and later in helping to organise wide support during the transition to democracy in the early 1990s.

Absence of Organised Socio–Economic Interest Groups at Independence

The colonial government did not have economic structures and policies conducive to the formation of African special–interest groups. At Independence, the urban population was tiny (5 per cent) even by the standards of neighbouring countries. The colonial administration did not invest much in manufacturing and Europeans mainly owned what little existed. Europeans also almost exclusively owned the agricultural estates, a major form of private ownership. Their lands, the most suitable for production of high–value crops, yielded 14 per cent of marketed output and 30 per cent of crop exports. The Marketing Board had monopsony power over the purchase and export of major crops; it discriminated against estates. Asians mostly dominated domestic trade. Insufficient social spending, poor conditions of African labour on the estates and the lack of alternatives to communal farming, which often did not even meet subsistence needs, forced Africans to seek wage work in neighbouring countries. All these conditions removed any basis for the emergence of African special–interest organisations.

Nyasaland had no national identity before colonial rule, but African opposition grew in reaction to high taxes and unpopular colonial economic policies. The Nyasaland African Congress (NAC) was formed primarily by the missionary–educated elite, urban dwellers, civil servants and rural entrepreneurs, as a council of Native Associations to oppose federation with Rhodesia. Although too weak to prevent that, the NAC nevertheless effected a constitutional change in 1955, leading to the creation of five posts for Africans in the Legislative Council. Some independence activists occupied these posts and used the Council to attack the Federation. After 1958, although Dr. Banda led an active but non–violent independence movement, his speeches throughout the country resulted in violence and disorder. Increasing tensions led the colonial government to recognise the inevitability of a power transition and to permit establishment of the Malawi Congress Party (MCP) in 1959, an outgrowth of the banned NAC and led by Dr. Banda. The MCP won the first national elections in 1961 and the democratic elections in 1964 with decisive victories.

The NAC and later the MCP recruited traditional leaders and placed great emphasis on rural and migrant workers. Although colonial rule encouraged African trade unionism in the 1950s to avoid worker militancy (there were four unions at Independence), and allowed producer and consumer co–operatives to form in order to monitor civil society, the MCP remained cautious of independent organisations. During the independence struggle, all societal organisations converged, at the expense of their individual identities, for a unified effort.

After Independence, the absence of special–interest groups and different political party organisations helped the MCP to impose its absolute leadership in the organisation of civil society. Through legislation, it solidified its power by forcing civil organisations to affiliate with the MCP. Thus, although represented on the Wage Advisory Board, the ill–organised trade unions had little or no say in wage policy. The MCP dismissed Cabinet members who contradicted its economic policies by advocating economic diversification and opposing private property. It heavily discouraged formation of foreign business or other special–interest groups. To limit competition and to avoid the formation of power centres, it restrained strong groups of European and Asian wholesale traders initially to 70 local–government centres and urban areas (1968) and eventually to only four cities (1978). In 1993, there were five industry–wide trade unions with no plant or enterprise representation (World Bank, 1993a) and decentralised bargaining. In the formal sector, about 12 per cent of the labour force, only about 5 per cent belonged to the unions; they accounted for less than 1 per cent of the labour force.

Poor Education and the Lack of Socio–Economic and Political Power

The generally high correlation between education, on the one hand, and democracy and civil rights on the other[7] indicates that the education patterns in Malawi deserve particular attention. Malawi inherited few educated people after the penurious social spending under colonial rule. It also suffered from the departure of large numbers of skilled expatriates, despite Dr. Banda's conciliatory position towards them. Although Scottish missionaries had achieved a primary–school enrolment rate slightly above the average in other British colonies, higher education was grossly inadequate to Africanise the civil service and other key posts after Independence.

The budgetary share of education spending rose after Independence but remained lower than in many neighbouring countries[8]. Later, the negative economic shocks of the mid–1980s led to its deterioration, from 16 per cent in 1964–71 to about 10 per cent in the 1980s. In 1993, education spending was only 3 per cent of GDP, compared to 5 per cent in Zambia, 7 per cent in Zimbabwe and 8 per cent in Botswana. Primary education received the greatest emphasis, but its quality declined, due to both the budget constraints and a 4.8 per cent annual growth rate in the school–age population after the mid–1980s. Regional disparities in educational quality (Table 6.1) depended mainly on the geographic distribution of the missionaries. Secondary and higher education spending also increased for a few years after Independence, but remained below targets thereafter[9]. The poor status of education resulted not merely from budgetary constraints, but also from the wage, employment and development policies of the government. When it adopted an agricultural growth strategy with a paramount role for the estates, cheap labour, ensured by low education, became necessary. Access to higher education was also largely uneven, with some vocational schools devoted exclusively to training members of the MYP.

Table 6.1. **Primary Schooling Indicators by Region, 1992**

	Net Enrolment Rates	Pupil/Teacher Ratios	Ratios of Unqualified Teachers
Northern	84	58	10
Central	52	72	9
Southern	51	70	18

The educational superiority of the Northern Region manifested itself in the leadership of the independence movement as well as in the emergence of political opposition after Independence. The younger and better–educated elite played a large role in the movement and in the decision to invite Dr. Banda to lead it as an old, experienced and respected figure. Yet his policies of slow Africanisation, introduction of hospital fees and not accommodating demands for civil–service wage increases disappointed this educated, urban elite, which organised major opposition against him in 1964–65. Northerners, the relatively greater proportion of this population, frequently were silenced by the MCP for opposing the rural emphasis of the development strategy. They thus generated a potential for political opposition. Between 1975 and 1976, 300 northerners were dismissed from their civil–service posts and imprisoned. Another, similar round of dismissals occurred in 1980. Conflict between this group, mainly from the Northern Region, and the Central Region, where most rural development programmes were implemented, partly accounts for the division of political constituencies along regional lines during the 1990s.

With the change of the political environment in 1994, emphasis on education increased drastically; real education spending rose three–fold and primary education outlays rose by a factor of 4.3. Spending on primary education now constitutes 71 per cent of total education spending, as opposed to 45 per cent earlier. Moreover, between the fiscal years 1992/93 and 1994/95, abolishing primary school fees led to a 60 per cent increase in gross enrolment rates, mostly in the relatively backward Central and Southern Regions.

Post–Independence Elements of Political Stability

Development strategy and economic policies that targeted growth through estate development mainly benefited small party and bureaucratic groups and resulted in only limited industrialisation and urbanisation. These small groups also largely solidified state control. Relatively good economic management and macroeconomic stability, coupled with Malawi's conciliatory approach to the West, also enabled continued donor support until the 1980s in order to maintain economic stability. Thus, although Banda's regime lacked political consensus, both socio–economic and political control mechanisms and donor–assisted economic stability contributed to an apparent political stability.

Legal and Administrative Elements of Political Stability

From Dr. Banda's return to Malawi in 1958 until the new Constitution of 1963 and Independence in July 1964, the MCP emerged as one of the best–organised and most powerful political parties in Africa. The MCP, the United Federal Party and the Congress Liberation Party all contested the election, but the other two obtained little African backing compared to the MCP. The victory derived from Dr. Banda's popularity, supported by both the party propaganda newspaper, *Malawi News*, and the MCP's youth groups, which discouraged the participation of other African parties. In the following years, Dr. Banda gradually established and intensified mechanisms of political repression. The Constitution was revised to declare the MCP as the only legitimate political party with Dr. Banda as its President.

President Banda's administration did not foster rapid Africanisation, both because few qualified Africans were available and because it could have generated a potential for nepotism. At Independence, only 33 Malawian university graduates lived in the country (American University, 1985). Dr. Banda placed two Europeans in his first Cabinet and assumed the responsibility of several ministerial portfolios himself. The Cabinet also contained more militant ministers, younger than he, who had paved the way for his leadership in the independence movement[10].

Both to tap expatriate expertise and to achieve continuity in the administration, Dr. Banda encouraged the expatriate population to remain in the country. Africanisation of the civil service was governed by strict qualification criteria that necessitated appropriate educational backgrounds; by 1965, Malawians held more than one–third of the senior positions, including 60 out of the 127 in the administrative service. In addition, 420 civil servants were sent overseas under government scholarships in training for high–ranking positions. Nevertheless, in 1971, 900 British remained in the top civil–service positions, as against 133 Malawians. Even in 1994, expatriates still held a significant portion of key technical and professional positions.

Various social groups had great expectations from Independence. The mission–educated or foreign–trained elite that had played a role in bringing Dr. Banda back and in helping organise the movement expected to obtain positions vacated after colonial rule, along with their benefits. Small–scale farmers expected the cessation of taxes and credit on demand. Dr. Banda's policies of slow Africanisation, limited response to civil–service wage demands, the introduction of hospital fees and strong diplomatic links with white–minority regimes abroad disappointed the groups involved in the independence movement. The educated elite started a hostile opposition because they also felt that he did not let them exercise power within their own ministerial portfolios. Among these voices, Henry Chipembere gathered a strong following in the Southern Region, including disgruntled civil servants and others. When the Cabinet split and dismissals and resignations of dissident ministers evolved into revolts in 1964, Dr. Banda banned public meetings in the Southern Region and placed the ministers under restriction. Chipembere escaped and organised an unsuccessful uprising in 1965. About 1 000 of his supporters were detained for extended periods while Chipembere himself fled to the United States.

Following these events, Dr. Banda maintained close ties with local institutions and traditional groups to enhance his single–handed, direct administrative control. This also positioned him directly against public opposition in local administrative matters and led to several constitutional changes to suppress dissent by limiting civil rights and freedoms. Among the most important of these were the Prevention Detention Order in 1964 which continued repressive measures of the colonial period; the Malawi Young Pioneer Act of 1965, which set up and began training the paramilitary youth wing of the MCP; the Trade–Union Registration and Trade Disputes Settlement Act of 1965, amended in 1968, which put restrictions on strike action and made necessary the affiliation of unions with the MCP; the Preservation Security Act of 1966 which gave broad delegation of authority to the armed and police forces; and the Penal Code, amended in 1973, which prohibited publications, limited journalism and thus contributed to the intellectual decline[11].

Malawi became a one–party state in 1966. To deal with splits in the Cabinet, the new Constitution explicitly mentioned the principles of "unity, loyalty, obedience and discipline", and expressed the major duty of the Government as the advancement of the welfare of the people. Meanwhile, the MCP party constitution was also revised to complement the Republican Constitution. Further amendments to the Constitution in 1968 gave absolute discretionary powers to the President over the appointment and dismissal of civil servants and government employees, including military officers. An amendment in 1971 made Dr. Banda President for his lifetime.

While the President viewed the educated minority with caution, he placed strong trust in rural people and the party's youth groups, especially the MYP, whose purpose was to conduct social and development work besides acting as a paramilitary force[12]. The MYP (headed by Aleke Banda) consisted of young men and women who trained intensively to work in agricultural and settlement schemes and trade schools, as well as to expand the influence of MCP, maintain control in politically unstable areas and inform the President about potential unrest. MYP was much larger than either the army or the police, also mostly loyal to Dr. Banda, and received a large share of the defence budget. Although small, these forces were well trained by the British and effective against the weak and diffused opposition. Expatriates initially dominated both and were replaced by Malawians only slowly as they gradually became suitably trained. The MYP gradually became a special security force for President Banda, complementing the army and police and immune to police arrest. Selected members of MYP were given three years of military training; some later appeared as over–enthusiastic in their security role and engaged in violent acts against citizens. A long rivalry between the MYP on the one hand and the army and police on the other surfaced during the transition to a multi–party system in the early 1990s. MYP members have caused major instability since then by launching raids from Mozambique where they went into hiding.

Dr. Banda used his discretionary powers to deal with potential political challenge by creating high turnover in government and party posts. Limited political mobility and few opportunities for employment in general ensured heavy competition for political posts, contributed to the turnover and raised the stakes associated with the high risk of dismissal. The average ministerial term of office averaged two and a half years in 1964–81. In the same period, 150 political appointees were expelled and publicly humiliated, and 40 ended in political detention (Mtewa, 1983). Disapproval of Dr. Banda's foreign policies, including dependence on foreign aid and the maintenance of relations with neighbouring white–minority regimes, continued to provoke opposition, especially among a new generation of public figures. In 1967, the security forces killed a former cabinet minister who led a small rebel movement; eight others were executed. In 1973–76, a series of anti–government plots were discovered. Political tensions then eased somewhat between 1977 and 1982, as the secret police kept control, leading to the release from prison of many detainees.

Ambitions to succeed Dr. Banda, who was ageing, also received severe reaction. In 1973, Aleke Banda, one of his strong supporters during the revolts of 1964–65, earned dismissal for publicly mentioning that he would consider succeeding Dr. Banda. In 1983, Dick Matanje, who led a relatively more consensus–building and popular wing of the MCP, and two other key political figures died in a car crash, leading to rumours that their deaths were not accidental but part of efforts to eliminate potential successors to Dr. Banda.

The district was the lowest level of national administration. Popular elections chose district councillors until 1966, but afterwards the MCP's district organisations selected them[13]. District conferences represented all local interest groups, namely the League of Malawi Women, the League of Malawi Youth — themselves organs of the MCP — and all of the district's recognised chiefs and sub–chiefs (American University, 1985). Because local interest groups were also represented by state–affiliated organisations, the selection process generated only an appearance of popular participation, to prevent political opposition from arising.

The state largely controlled the judiciary and the press. A 1962 change had clearly separated the role of the chiefs from that of the executive by replacing the chiefs' courts with the Local Court system. It effectively repealed the colonial decision to strengthen the chiefs' roles in the 1930s. In 1969, however, the Local Courts Amendment Act allowed traditional courts to try criminal cases, provided that they used British law. The rules of evidence nevertheless were less strict and secret trials were possible. This put some trials under political influence, especially as the re-creation of traditional courts indebted some chiefs to the President for their posts, and because the Justice Minister allocated cases to specific courts. The press became an important organ to spread and maintain the popularity of the MCP. Two of the three newspapers after Independence were the MCP's own; the third, expatriate-owned, remained subject to MCP censorship. The MCP further strengthened its direct control over the press and radio in 1973 (Williams, 1978).

Economic Elements of Political Stability

Economic Structure and Development Strategy. Agriculture, the single largest sector at Independence, remained the main emphasis of development policies. It produced 40 per cent of GDP in 1970 and 35 per cent in 1995 (in 1978 prices), while industry's share remained roughly constant at around 18 per cent throughout the post–Independence period. In 1987, agriculture employed 87 per cent of the labour force (only 5 per cent of that was formal–sector employment) and industry about 5 per cent. Agricultural exports provided more than 80 per cent of total export earnings (goods and non–factor services) in most years after 1980[14].

Agriculture displayed a highly bifurcated structure which differentiated the estate and smallholder sub–sectors based on tenure and production rights, irrespective of size (Table 6.2). This dualism, created during the colonial period, became institutionalised in the Land Act of 1967. Smallholders cultivated communal lands, with no management or ownership rights; tenure on the estates was either freehold or leasehold for up to 99 years. The Act also gave the executive the right to determine crops grown on communal lands and to convert communal lands to leaseholds, weakening the traditional role of the chiefs in land allocation.

Although development policies initially emphasised investment in the smallholder sub–sector, they mainly favoured smallholders, especially the largest 20 per cent, already in more advantageous positions of access to credit and infrastructure. The first rural development programmes and the National Rural Development Program in 1978 both failed to improve conditions for the majority of smallholders and led to greater inequalities among them. In 1980, the top 23 per cent of smallholders (with more than two hectares per household) accounted for 76 per cent, 60 per cent and 38 per cent of the communal land devoted to tobacco, cotton and maize, respectively, while the poorest 77 per cent (with less than 1.5 hectare per household) produced the rest. Average incomes also varied greatly; in 1980, the incomes of the top 23 per cent ranged between 343 Malawian Kwacha (MK) and 805 MK, while the poorer smallholders earned only between 91 MK and 268 MK (Mhone, 1992)[15].

Table 6.2. **Land Distribution by Tenure and Region**
(in thousand hectares)

	Population		Total Land Area	Agricultural Land	Estate Land		Customary Land		Customary Land per capita
	1966	1989			1978	1989	1978	1989	1989
North	498	966	2 693	696	97	105	492	590	0.61
Central	1 475	3 319	3 559	1 878	240	569	1 216	1 309	0.39
South	2 067	4 215	3 175	1 767	133	174	1 167	1 593	0.38

Source: World Bank (1995*b*) and Pryor (1988).

After the First Development Plan (1962–65), the Government shifted its emphasis to the estate sector, deciding that it would become the engine of economic growth with the smallholders as its source of cheap labour. Although this shift followed a poor maize harvest and year–to–year fluctuations in smallholder tobacco output, and was based on efficiency grounds, the superior productivity of the estates over the smallholders sector remained unsubstantiated (Media Discussion Paper, 1989). Nonetheless, between 1970 and 1993 about 23 000 new estates were established (mostly in the Southern and Central Regions where the land is more suitable for cultivation), while their mean size fell from 345 hectares to 50 hectares (World Bank, 1995*b*).

The encroachment of the estates produced substantial population pressure on smallholder farms, especially in the historically more densely populated Southern Region where about half the population dwells. In 1985, average income per household in the Southern Region was about half of that in the Northern and Central Regions. Net migration occurred from both the Northern and Southern Regions to the Central Region starting in the 1960s. By 1992, the estates occupied only 20 per cent of the cultivated land, but the most productive part of it. They produced 9 per cent of GDP, 35 per cent of agricultural output and 90 per cent of exports. Smallholders farmed the less fertile 80 per cent of the cultivated land, but created about 25 per cent of GDP and 65 per cent of agricultural output (World Bank, 1995*b*).

Redistributive Policies and Institutions of State Control. Overall economic performance during the 15 years after Independence showed promise, with an average annual real GDP growth of 5.8 per cent and per capita GDP growth of 3 per cent (Figure 6.1). From 1965 to 1973, real GDP growth (5.9 per cent per year) matched the average of sub–Saharan Africa, but from 1973 to 1980 Malawi's average real growth of 5.3 per cent was twice that of sub–Saharan Africa. This performance was especially impressive because Malawi is land–locked and it lacked skilled labour, mineral resources and a developed infrastructure at Independence. The driving force was export growth in tea, tobacco and sugar, which averaged 4.5 per cent, 13.7 per cent and 24 per cent respectively between 1973 and 1980. The share of total exports, 60 per cent in 1968, rose to 85 per cent by 1988, when tobacco alone held 64 per cent[16] (Sahn and Arulpragasam, 1991).

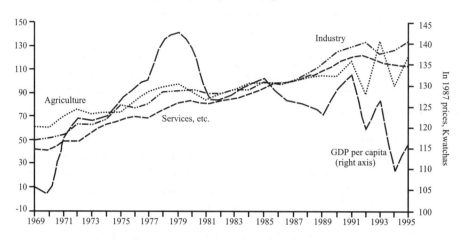

Promotion of the estate sector and tobacco production using cheap labour and discriminatory redistribution from smallholders through the Agricultural Development and Marketing Company (ADMARC)[17] greatly helped this performance. Post–Independence production and marketing policies as well as the development strategy accentuated the dual agricultural structure by clearly favouring estate development. Smallholders were prohibited from producing high–value crops, such as barley and tobacco, until 1990. While the estates could export their produce at market prices, smallholders had to go through ADMARC, which paid them only a portion of the actual export price — 63 per cent in 1964–69, 42 per cent in 1970–80 and 49 per cent in 1980–84 (Pryor, 1990; Mhone, 1992). ADMARC's marketing operations generated profits throughout the 1970s[18], and 76 per cent of its investment spending went to the estates between 1972 and 1981 (Gulhati, 1989). In 1978, half of ADMARC's investment and loans supported tobacco and only 4.3 per cent helped the peasant sector (Kydd and Christiansen, 1982).

ADMARC's control of one–fifth of the assets of the Industrial Development Bank (INDEBANK) also helped channel resources to the estate sector (Pryor, 1990). Between 1964 and 1984, the estates' share of total agricultural production rose from 16 per cent to 42 per cent and that of exports from 26 per cent to 66 per cent. Total employment in the estate sector increased from 51 000 (about a third of total formal employment) in 1968 to 181 000 in 1980 (about half of total formal employment) (Gulhati, 1989).

Conversions of communal land to leaseholds and master–farmer programmes also worked as a mechanism to enhance political control. Estate–development policy tried to generate an economic elite that would provide political support for the regime. Dr. Banda particularly encouraged bureaucrats and politicians to become estate owners. During the 1970s, estate expansion occurred mainly through master–farmer programmes and credit policies, mostly on commercial principles. Generally profitable, the estates benefited largely the educated urban elite. The economic downturn of the 1980s and increased state control, however, brought increasing abuses. According to a survey in 1986, 19 per cent of the estate owners were politicians and civil servants, 36 per cent were mostly former smallholders and the rest had high to medium job status (Pryor, 1990). In 1993, the number of estate owners was an estimated 30 000, about one–sixtieth of the total number of farmers.

Wage and labour policies, as well, redistributed resources from smallholders to the estates. They also prevented economic diversification and urbanisation. Between 1970 and 1992, average real wages declined by more than 40 per cent (World Bank, 1993a), as minimum wages were adjusted to inflation only occasionally[19]. Higher real incomes suffered more than lower ones, so that income inequalities between the rural and urban dwellers and among civil servants narrowed[20]. Although the ratio of rural to urban real minimum wages rose from 61 per cent in 1970 to 80 per cent in 1992, the average rural–urban wage differential did not improve as much because minimum wages were more binding for estate employment than in the rest of the formal sector; the ratio of rural to urban wages in general rose only to 28 per cent in 1985 from 24 per cent in 1968.

Although minimum wage policy discouraged urban migration and the manufacturing sector was heavily concentrated, the urban population nonetheless increased to about 15 per cent of the total by 1995 from only about 5 per cent at Independence. Despite this high rate of urbanisation, the urban population has remained proportionally very small even by regional standards[21]. Given the low incomes of smallholders, a large proportion of which fell even below subsistence levels[22], and the lack of domestic job alternatives, significant labour migration occurred (especially to South Africa) to seek wage employment[23]. Some 25 per cent of the labour force worked abroad in 1972 (Pryor, 1990). The 250 000 migrants in 1974 roughly equalled total formal employment in that year (World Bank, 1993a). The absence of men from their localities for long periods also helped to prevent the organisation of local interest groups.

Nationalisation of the commercial banks[24] also greatly enhanced Government control over the economy. Although the Government did not nationalise much else[25], the Industrial Development Act of 1966 vested it with power to command the industrial sector. Industry became largely concentrated in a few parastatals and a few large multinational companies. The largest parastatals were ADMARC, MDC (Malawi Development Corporation, established in 1964 to promote private industrial entrepreneurship) and the Press Company (established in 1960 as an investment holding company fully owned by Dr. Banda and used for subsidising first the NAC and later the MCP). The Press Company obtained credits from the state–owned commercial banks and ADMARC, and acquired a significant number of estates leased to high–ranking officials and bureaucrats. By 1980, Press Holding housed more than 8 500 large commercial farms (Chipeta in Mhone, 1992). In the early 1980s, the public sector and

Press Holding owned about 30 per cent of the estate land. These properties accounted for about 30 per cent of employment on the estates and 2.5 per cent of the economically active population in agriculture (Pryor, 1990). Malawi's largest single employer, Press Holding had more than 30 per cent of manufacturing employment and 10 per cent of total formal–sector employment in 1980 (Pryor, 1990).

Post–Independence economic policies and institutions largely favoured the interests of a small bureaucratic or party elite through the concentrated industrial structure, bound it to the MCP's centralised power and thus helped prevent an elite political opposition from emerging. Price controls, exclusive licensing, restrictive rules and regulations, and inadequate credit all generally discouraged entry[26], as did barriers to the regional concentration of industry. Because the proceeds of labour–intensive manufacturing went mainly to expand the state sector and the Press Company, rural areas hardly benefited. From the late 1970s, although emphasis on small and medium–scale manufacturing increased, with commercial banks and other institutions established to promote it, credit constraints, collateral demands and a lack of inter–industry linkages all discouraged industrial diversification[27].

To summarise, while legal and institutional measures prevented special–interest groups from forming, the economic structure and redistributive policies did not bring broad–based political support for the government. Economic policies targeted growth *via* development of the estate sector and a concentrated industrial structure, which almost exclusively benefited a small group of bureaucratic and party elite. The Government chiefly controlled manufacturing and had command of opportunities for private employment. It pursued wage policies that discouraged urbanisation and thus reduced the potential for a large, urban–based political opposition. Land scarcity and failure to attain food self–sufficiency (intensified by an inflow of Mozambican refugees) led to a large labour migration to neighbouring countries. This eroded ethnic and community relations, and again mitigated the potential for political opposition to emerge within the labour force. Concentration on a limited number of primary export commodities, however, especially with export gains not distributed to the larger society, aggravated the vulnerability of the economy to exogenous shocks and should have increased the potential for political opposition.

External Elements of Political Stability

After Independence, Dr. Banda tried to keep highly qualified personnel in the civil service and the Government, which implied preserving at least initially the posts of experienced, well–trained expatriates. Because land–locked Malawi very much needed regional economic co–operation, he also maintained good diplomatic and economic relations with the white–minority governments of the region, despite criticisms of the front–line states. All this made Malawi the only western–aligned, African–ruled country in southern Africa. The number and regional variety of foreign embassies were distinctive in the region; they reflected linkages with places like Israel, Chinese Taipei and South Korea that contributed to several agricultural projects. Malawi also pursued relatively liberal trade polices and established a limited version of a market economy until the 1980s; tariffs were much lower than in comparable countries (although the tariff structure was similar, with higher rates on primary goods) and quantitative restrictions were deliberately avoided to prevent incentives for corruption, especially given the limited qualified personnel to administer them.

Until the end of 1970s, Malawi benefited from favourable terms of trade as well and a global embargo on Rhodesian tobacco exports. Declining terms of trade in the late 1970s, however, severely affected the economy, leading to current account deficits of 30 per cent of GDP (before grants) in 1979 and 25 per cent in 1980 (Figure 6.2). Between 1977 and 1983 the debt–to–GDP ratio rose by 70 per cent, the debt–service ratio tripled[28] and international reserves declined from three months of imports to less than two weeks. Worker migration and remittances fell due to a downturn in the mineral markets, oil shocks and the resulting slowdown in the neighbouring countries. The conversion of land to leaseholds and estates, coupled with the high rate of population growth, had generated a land problem, which the Government's ban on labour migration to South Africa between 1974 to 1977 had further intensified[29]. Droughts in 1980 and 1981 further aggravated the downturn and necessitated large maize imports.

Given its lack of involvement in regional disputes and its apparently stable domestic politics, Malawi kept military spending below the average of the region, at roughly 2 or 3 per cent of GDP, although it rose to about 5 per cent in 1979 and 1980. By the 1990s, it had gradually decreased to around 1 per cent (US ACDA, 1994). In the Government budget, military outlays climbed from 2 to 3 per cent during the 1960s to more than 10 per cent in 1980, then fell to less than 5 per cent by the 1990s[30].

Instability in neighbouring countries, particularly Mozambique, substantially affected the Malawi economy. Although they never posed a direct threat to domestic stability, frequent incursions by Portuguese forces across Malawi's borders in search of members of FRELIMO harmed villagers and businessmen. The most significant influence on the economy came later, however, during the Mozambican civil war, when transport costs leaped to about 30 per cent of import value between 1976 and 1980 and to more than 50 per cent between 1981 and 1984, when Mozambique's ports at Beira and Ncala were finally closed. Malawi was especially vulnerable because 90 per cent of its trade passed through Mozambique and almost all of it had to be redirected through South Africa. The war in Mozambique also brought an estimated 300 000 refugees to Malawi by 1987, over 1 million by 1990 and a still–high 600 000 by 1996. Increased social and military spending to accommodate the refugees exacerbated the economic problems.

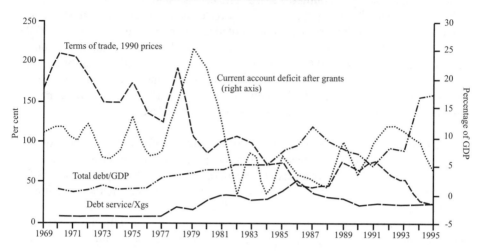

Figure 6.2. **Current Account Balance, Foreign Debt, Debt Service and Terms of Trade**

Both the exogenous economic shocks and political instability in neighbouring countries aggravated the poverty of the majority of the population and contributed to a now–increasing potential for political instability in Malawi. While economic management remained prudent enough not to lose control over the macroeconomic balances, the impact of declining financial resources fell mainly on investment spending, specifically on primary education, and on wage earnings. Malawi's access to foreign financing helped to avert the full force of these threats until the 1990s.

Although foreign donors did not particularly reward Malawi's liberal trade and regional policies[31], the country did enjoy a continuous flow of donor aid throughout the post–Independence period, although the multilateral component has increased its weight since the 1980s. The donor community approved not only of Malawi's relatively open economy with few price controls but also of the enabling environment created by its apparent political stability. Central decision making by an authoritative government without major organised opposition also permitted considerable efficiency in implementing donor–advised policies. Considering that political stability and good economic performance generally interlink, continued donor aid thus appears to have helped postpone the awakening of threats to political stability that lay dormant.

Emergence of Threats to Political Stability and Transition to Democracy

Immediately following Independence, Dr. Banda's economic, social and foreign policies provoked opposition among those who had initiated the independence movement. In response, he turned to measures of severe political repression both to suppress that opposition and to maintain the largely discriminatory development policies intact. For many years, favourable terms of trade allowed achievement of an impressive

166

growth performance through the 1970s, but the exogenous shocks of the late 1970s and the ensuing economic downturn revealed the weaknesses in domestic economic management, particularly the lack of diversification and import dependence.

Both the concentration of political and economic power in the hands of a small elite and the emphasis of development strategy on a limited base of primary exports increased the vulnerability of economic performance to exogenous shocks and thus reduced the effectiveness of political control mechanisms. Notwithstanding its relatively liberal trade policies and significant private sector, Malawi was hardly a market economy because its redistributive policies greatly discriminated against smallholders and small–scale manufacturing. The development strategy and economic policies impeded economic diversification and sustainable growth, while social spending remained inadequate to redress colonial neglect. As the exogenous shocks accentuated the economy's inherent problems, incomes badly deteriorated. Per capita GDP[32] plunged 25 per cent between 1980 and 1987. Increasing inequality accompanied rising poverty[33].

The efforts to prevent an elite opposition from emerging also led to inefficiencies in economic management. The allocation of some of the newly created estates to the bureaucratic and party elite, who knew little about farming, offers an example. The decline in the terms of trade and the overvaluation of the exchange rate in the mid–1980s reduced the estates' profitability and led to growing opposition by estate owners as a class. Although generally run on commercial principles, the public sector and Press Holding had quasi–governmental services and were closely linked with the estate and financial sectors. As the overall economic situation deteriorated, major parastatals and Press Holding ran large losses[34]. The increase in commercial bank lending to estates throughout the late 1980s, with a decline in lending to industry, reflected not only policy but also the increasing losses of this sector.

The Government secured four loan agreements with the IMF and four with the World Bank between 1979 and 1987, plus two Paris Club debt reschedulings, while the foreign–aid flow held up during the 1980s. The IFI lending programmes succeeded in that social indicators, such as school enrolment and life expectancy rates, rose[35]. MDC, Press Holding and to a lesser degree ADMARC were restructured. Tax revenues increased. Despite political resistance from the private sector, Dr. Banda implemented large increases in smallholder crop prices to build a strategic food reserve. This initially generated a positive supply response but failed to prevent a real decline in the relative price of maize. Tariff increases took place and foreign–exchange licensing persisted. The overvaluation of the currency in the 1980s mainly benefited urban consumers and civil servants.

To achieve the reform targets on financial balances, the government mainly reduced its investment spending (Figure 6.3), rather than restructuring the economy to enhance production potential; in 1984, the share of gross domestic investment in GDP was about one–third that in 1978. The severe decline in real incomes, accompanied by increasing inequalities, led to a rising potential for social unrest. The World Bank and IMF programmes, based on intensive consultations, may have helped increase the awareness of such problems among domestic economic managers, given that the centralised political culture usually did not otherwise allow civil servants and politicians to discuss them with the President.

Figure 6.3. **Gross Domestic Saving, Gross Domestic Investment and Consumption** (percentage of GDP)

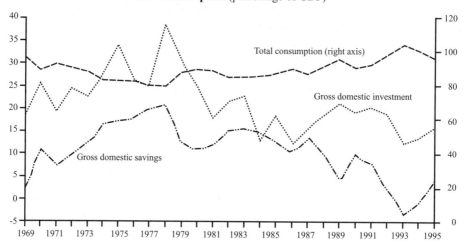

Throughout the post–Independence period, frequent dissolution and reorganisation of the Government prevented politicians from forming power bases, and candidates to succeed Dr. Banda usually faced harsh measures. Exile groups, however, mostly in the front–line states, did form several opposition parties, among them the Socialist League of Malawi (LESOMA), the Malawi Freedom Movement (MAFREMO) and the Malawi Democratic Union (MDU). A number of incidents have occurred since the late 1970s, associated with repressive MCP measures against this rising potential for political opposition. They included a letter bomb sent to the leader of LESOMA, admittedly on Dr. Banda's instructions, followed by his mysterious death in 1983; the life imprisonment of the leader of MAFREMO and his wife, also in 1983; the killing of a senior official of MAFREMO and nine others by a fire bomb in Zambia in 1989; and the exile or imprisonment of several others.

Opposition activity by the leaders in exile intensified in the early 1990s. In 1991, the Malawi Socialist Labour Party was formed in Tanzania; in 1992, a former senior official of MCP, Muluzi, formed the United Democratic Front (UDF); again in 1992, following the first conference of 80 political exiles gathered in Lusaka to initiate political reform, a Lusaka–based United Front for Multi–Party Democracy (UFMD) — a merger of LESOMA, MAFREMO and MDU — formed under the leadership of the exiled former trade–union leader, Chakufwa Chihana. UFMD later became the

Alliance for Democracy (AFORD). Although the front–line states sympathised with this opposition and housed many political exiles, they took no significant diplomatic or political positions against Dr. Banda. Their most evident form of support for the opposition appeared as critical writings in the Zambian press, especially during the transition to democracy, which coincided with Zambia's.

In the absence of any civil–society organisation or a political leader to mobilise effective internal opposition, the church functioned as the most effective and widely based institutional vehicle of expression. In 1989, the Pope visited Malawi, emphasising human rights and democracy. As poverty became a common unifying theme within the rural sector, the Roman Catholic Church in 1992 issued a pastoral letter that emphasised growing inequality and the poor status of education, health and human rights. Some 16 000 copies of this letter went both to urban churches and to the rural churches, where Dr. Banda derives much support — a major break from the past because the Church previously regarded Dr. Banda as a strong spiritual leader and the sole political one.

The return of Chihana to Malawi and his immediate detention received wide publicity and became one in a series of events that displayed internationally the increasing human–rights abuses of the MCP Government. International donors eventually suspended all non–humanitarian aid. This, coupled with drought in 1992, deepened the political crisis and led to industrial unrest, especially in the Southern Region, strikes, urban and student demonstrations and riots. Finally, following a joint call for multi–party democracy by a council of churches, Dr. Banda reluctantly agreed to hold a referendum late in 1992.

The referendum produced a 67 per cent turnout with 63 per cent of the votes in favour of democratic elections. The Southern and Northern Regions mainly governed this outcome, as the Central Region, where Dr. Banda remained the most influential political and religious leader, remained largely loyal. Even the Church, which had played so instrumental a role in the organisation of a political reform movement across the country, abstained from criticising him in the Central Region. In the subsequent 1994 elections, UDF leader Muluzi was elected President by 47.3 per cent of the votes, Dr. Banda received 33.6 per cent and Chihana received 18.6 per cent. The breakdown of votes among the political parties broadly coincided with the administrative regions. It reflected an absence of both distinctive party ideologies and significant ethnic rivalries. AFORD won mostly in the Northern Region, MCP in the Central Region and UDF in the most populous and poorest Southern Region. AFORD emerged mainly as a party of intellectuals from the Northern Region. It did not at first form a coalition with the UDF, but worked with the MCP, leaving the UDF to form a minority government with only some MCP elements. After a cabinet reshuffle later in 1994 made Chihana the second Vice–President and gave AFORD four ministries, AFORD and UDF formed a coalition government.

Conclusions: The Prospects for Political Stability

Retrospective: The MCP Legacy

Dr. Banda's excessive political powers enabled apparent political stability and a reasonably well–managed economy in Malawi for almost three decades after its Independence. Production and ownership remained under the direct control of either the state or Dr. Banda. Although a private sector existed, estate ownership and industrial licences went mostly to the party and bureaucratic elite as rewards for loyalty to Dr. Banda. Development and redistribution policies aimed to create an economic elite that supported the MCP regime, but made the economy vulnerable. External shocks, droughts and the negative effects of regional factors during the 1980s aggravated poverty and inequality, which resulted in a growing opposition to the repressive MCP regime. Progressively losing control over this mounting opposition, the system gave way in 1992–94. Constitutional changes in 1994 and 1995, part of the transition to democracy, ended one–party rule and the discretionary control of Dr. Banda, abolished the traditional–court system and established a free press. In 1994, the first multi–party elections in three decades since Independence took place.

Malawi has had a relatively well–managed economy due partly to the continued role of qualified expatriates and partly to the efficiencies of centralised decision making by Dr. Banda. Even during the economic downturn of the 1980s, budget deficits held to about 5 per cent of GDP, which was low by developing–country standards. Furthermore, relatively liberal international policies and the lack of major price distortions attracted continuous donor aid (except for the interruption in the early 1990s) and debt reschedulings. As a result, at the onset of market reforms in 1994, Malawi had a relatively sustainable level of debt (217 per cent of exports in net present–value terms, as against the 220 per cent threshold for severe indebtedness defined by the World Bank), although its debt service was slightly higher than comfortable.

Prospects

Maintaining relatively sustainable economic balances is important for making market reforms successful, eliminating poverty and thereby reducing potential political instability. Improvements in fiscal and current account balances since 1994 thus indicate improved prospects for economic stability as well as continued donor aid. Given that donors usually condition aid on the success of democratic reforms, continued progress on that front has importance for economic reforms.

The absence of civil–society organisations and a participatory political culture challenge the current government to find ways to establish and maintain democratic institutions. The overly centralised decision mechanism of the Banda regime severely deterred the development of an institutional capacity. Although the transition to a

170

multi–party system has allowed the emergence of unions and newspapers, they nevertheless often reflect the institutional structure of the former regime due to their close affiliations with the three existing political parties, rather than the independence they need and should have. The former regime's strong, influential medium of social control, radio broadcasting, continues as an important promotional tool of the incumbent government.

The concentrated industrial and estate sectors also pose challenges to implementing market reforms. The Press Company, 96 per cent of which Dr. Banda owned, is a large conglomerate that accounts for about 10 per cent of formal employment and 30 per cent of GDP. Its restructuring is important, not only to prevent the flow of funds to the MCP and thus to secure fair political competition, but also to establish a market mechanism to promote competition and efficiency rather than favouring the elite of the previous regime. The new Government intends to nationalise the Press Company, but this faces great resistance from MCP officials and might result in large economic losses from decapitalisation of its companies by their owners and managers.

The Government has already initiated major economic, legal and institutional reforms. Reforms to establish a market economy and achieve economic diversification will help generate socio–economic groups that could provide political support for them. The emergence of a small–scale, private entrepreneur class will be important for generating political support for market reforms and improving socio–economic conditions. Following the elections, donor agencies helped put substantial macroeconomic reforms in place rapidly: a new Banking Act; the revised Reserve Bank and Capital Market Development Acts, plus other institutional reforms to ensure the commitment to a liberal financial system; fiscal reforms, which included a broadened tax base and a major cut in the number of civil servants; and substantially eased foreign–trade restrictions and export–licensing requirements. To improve the status of the poor, all fees, charges and uniform requirements on primary school education have gone, resulting in a major increase in enrolment rates.

On the structural side, the shares of the Press Company in the two commercial banks were reduced from 40 per cent to 25 per cent, privatisations have started and restrictions on the marketing of smallholder cash crops *via* ADMARC have been lifted. As a result, smallholder agriculture and small manufacturing show signs of progress; in 1996, smallholder agricultural production was forecast to jump by 40 per cent. Substantial diversification into drought–resistant crops has been achieved and non–traditional exports were expected to rise by more than 20 per cent in 1996. Improved relations with donors and favourable weather conditions have also helped. While the long–term success of the reforms must yet emerge, the economy clearly has shown signs of improvement, including informal–sector growth which indicates that GDP growth may even have exceeded the preliminary figures of about 9 per cent in 1995 and 11 per cent in 1996. These developments could imply a growing base of political support for market reforms and democratic institutions, and thus point to increasing prospects for political stability.

Although political opposition to the repressive MCP regime was broad–based, the first democratic elections saw a divided political opposition to the MCP along the lines of the three administrative regions. Clear distinctions among the political parties with respect to either ideologies or economic policies have not appeared. In general, political balances do not yet appear as firmly established, and the prospect of a sustained coalition between the UDF and AFORD also remains clouded.

The MCP faces a looming leadership crisis. Dr. Banda, who had swayed the crowds with his powerful leadership and his role in the independence movement, is dead. The continued dominance of the MCP in the Central Region have depended on his personality and leadership. The balance of power thus may change with his replacement by the less popular John Tembo. Tembo was publicly suspected as responsible for the accident that killed several key political figures in 1983, allegedly to strengthen his potential for candidacy to succeed President Banda. The military has shown some hostility towards Tembo; in 1991 the Commander–in–Chief of the Malawi army resisted efforts to designate Tembo officially as the successor of Banda. The possibility of a weakening MCP leadership in the period to follow Dr. Banda might lead to a further shift of power to the opposition parties, especially the UDF.

Although party rivalries do not pose a direct threat to political stability, divisions in the opposition to the MCP, which still has a relatively firmly established political base, might slow the pace and reduce the success of reforms. Nevertheless, the former regime's development strategy and policies are so thoroughly discredited that they are hardly likely to be readopted, even if AFORD rejoins forces with the MCP. The elimination of the monopoly power of the Press conglomerate and its links with the financial system remains a major challenge for reforms. Moreover, a cloud hanging over economic reforms such as deregulation of marketing and trade involves a potential for conflict of interests between Malawians and the Asian traders hitherto dominant in trade. It might lead to increased social tension between the two groups.

The former military wing of the MCP, the MYP, has emerged as a major source of political instability. The decision to disarm the MYP led to clashes between the army and MYP in December 1993, sparking widespread unrest. The new constitution officially disbanded the MYP and its disarmament was completed in January 1994, but thousands of MYP members fled to Mozambique. Although Mozambique agreed to repatriate them, about 2 000 remained. Within Malawi, the threat to stability posed by former MYP members apparently peaked at the beginning of 1995. It may well diminish over time as they start to become involved in productive activities.

In summary, the first democratic government since Independence has initiated broad–based market reforms, including privatisation, fiscal reforms and market and price liberalisation. It has made a major effort to restructure the economy and to reform the institutions which thwarted economic diversification, sustainable growth and balanced development over three decades. Although much room remains for further progress, the reforms thus far have improved economic balances and donor relations.

As they succeed further, the financial and economic power of the MCP could weaken, potentially leading to a shift of its support to other parties. Irrespective of that, however, replacing the inherited economic and political institutions with market–based, democratic ones is crucial to generate a foundation for political reforms. Currently weak civil–society organisations, hobbled by the long post–Independence traditions, still do not generally display a sense of political freedom consistent with a democratic culture. In time, however, successful social, political and economic reforms likely will considerably reinforce each other. Economic diversification can play an especially important role in that process.

Annex 1. **Real Rates of Growth and Inflation**
(Per cent per year, in 1987 prices)

	GDP	Agriculture	Manufacturing	Per Capita GDP	CPI Inflation (yearly average)
1970	0.48	-1.32	..	-2.01	..
1971	16.22	16.85	..	13.41	..
1972	6.23	9.60	..	3.50	..
1973	2.30	-6.29	..	-0.26	..
1974	7.18	2.06	..	0.66	..
1975	6.09	0.92	..	3.25	..
1976	5.00	11.85	-3.70	2.46	..
1977	4.92	11.22	3.85	1.70	..
1978	9.75	2.93	4.69	7.04	..
1979	4.40	3.12	4.95	1.19	..
1980	0.41	-6.54	-0.22	-2.75	..
1981	-5.29	-8.20	3.60	-8.03	11.81
1982	2.50	6.40	-0.33	-0.99	9.82
1983	3.72	4.43	7.09	1.06	13.50
1984	5.36	5.80	2.44	1.97	20.03
1985	4.57	0.42	3.18	1.31	10.52
1986	-0.21	0.62	2.22	-3.23	14.05
1987	1.63	0.84	0.94	-1.36	25.18
1988	3.17	2.02	3.27	-0.16	33.88
1989	1.36	2.45	8.50	-2.06	12.46
1990	8.25	-0.25	11.25	4.73	11.50
1991	6.15	12.80	3.00	2.80	12.62
1992	-7.33	-25.12	2.98	-10.07	22.70
1993	9.70	52.98	-10.45	5.98	19.66
1994	-10.22	-29.31	3.15	-13.35	34.66
1995*	9.90	28.29	6.35	6.17	83.00

(*)   preliminary
Source: World Bank files.

Annex 2. Macroeconomic Indicators
(Percentage of GDP in current Malawi Kwachas, unless otherwise indicated)

	Consumption	Investment	Exports of GNFS	Imports of GNFS	Domestic Savings	Curr. Acc. Deficit (after grants)	Fiscal Deficit (after grants)	Debt	Debt Service in % of Exports (G&S)
1969		18.37	23.48	39.59	2.26	10.50	..	..	..
1970	89.18	25.73	24.25	39.16	10.82	11.98	..	42.13	7.78
1971	92.85	19.17	23.45	35.47	7.15	9.06	..	38.53	7.34
1972	90.26	24.39	23.29	37.94	9.74	12.08	..	40.51	8.05
1973	87.55	22.39	27.64	37.58	12.45	6.25	..	45.42	8.99
1974	83.62	27.32	28.02	38.96	16.38	6.51	..	41.85	7.78
1975	83.05	33.72	29.13	45.89	16.95	12.99	..	42.38	8.04
1976	82.17	26.26	30.44	38.87	17.83	6.37	..	44.62	9.07
1977	79.95	24.68	30.00	34.63	20.05	7.66	5.12	55.69	10.18
1978	79.48	38.44	23.19	41.11	20.52	..	5.76	..	19.51
1979	87.40	30.24	23.19	40.83	12.60	25.10	8.49	62.43	17.37
1980	89.21	24.74	24.84	38.80	10.78	20.98	8.39	66.32	27.67
1981	88.21	17.62	25.67	31.50	11.79	11.76	8.40	65.64	35.93
1982	84.92	21.40	22.50	28.82	15.08	..	6.09	72.60	35.69
1983	84.77	22.80	20.75	28.32	15.23	8.50	4.88	72.37	29.81
1984	85.18	12.88	28.37	26.43	14.82	-0.32	3.69	72.50	31.11
1985	87.12	18.59	24.19	29.90	12.88	6.38	4.52	89.97	39.63
1986	89.88	12.26	22.97	25.11	10.12	3.54	9.46	98.32	53.68
1987	86.72	15.68	25.94	28.34	13.28	2.60	7.96	118.26	38.26
1988	90.80	18.74	24.12	33.65	9.20	1.36	2.80	102.27	32.78
1989	95.28	21.16	19.63	36.07	4.72	9.07	2.92	93.60	32.25
1990	90.63	19.13	24.08	33.83	9.37	3.42	4.08	85.28	23.67
1991	92.10	20.15	23.54	35.78	7.90	8.75	3.31	70.93	25.29
1992	98.32	18.78	22.47	39.57	1.68	12.07	10.50	93.26	24.89
1993	103.30	12.19	16.45	31.94	-3.30	11.06	6.77	90.66	24.03
1994	100.53	13.23	28.90	43.00	-2.40	9.20	15.08	156.89	21.60
1995*	95.92	15.77	28.00	37.50	4.18	3.70	6.90	146.60	19.70

(*)   preliminary.
Source: World Bank files.

Notes

1. According to the census of 1966, Europeans were less than one half of 1 per cent of the total population in Malawi (American University, 1985).

2. Per capita GDP in 1965 was only half of that of sub–Saharan Africa and the infant mortality rate was 200 as opposed to 160 in sub–Saharan Africa (World Bank, 1989).

3. Based on estimates by the National Statistical Office in 1969 (Pryor, 1990).

4. For instance, the *Ngoni* in the North, who appeared as the most united among the chiefdoms, had to discontinue their own army force. In the 1930s, however, as the colonial administration moved towards a more indirect rule, local chiefs were given somewhat more autonomy, the judicial power of traditional courts became more formal and local revenue collection gained more importance.

5. More than one–third of the male labour force was outside the country in 1953 (American University, 1985).

6. Based on the number of service years between 1964 and 1983, the *Nyanja* and *Lomwe* were under–represented in the Cabinet (Pryor, 1990), while those from the Northern and Central regions were over–represented in the lower ranks of the police force and the southerners were over–represented in the higher ranks.

7. See, for example, Barro (1996).

8. The net primary enrolment rate was 66 per cent in 1992 whereas that of neighbouring countries was 81 per cent (World Bank, 1995c).

9. The secondary–school gross enrolment rate rose from 3 per cent in 1964 to about 5 per cent in the 1980s (World Bank, 1995c), while the average for the continent in 1965 was 5 per cent, rising to 20 per cent in 1986.

10. Chipembere and Chime led the more militant group of the independence movement. They were elected to the Legislative Council of the Federation in 1955 after a constitutional change that allowed the participation of five Africans, and initiated a hostile opposition

towards the Government. In fact, Banda's leadership of the NAC was intended to be ceremonial, to use his qualities to achieve the desired goal of real power for the African people.

11. According to Taylor and Bodice (1983), among the 144 countries of the world, Malawi ranked 124th with respect to political rights and 111th with respect to civil rights during 1973–79.

12. Delegation of military power to MYP also contributed to the revolts against Banda's policies in 1965.

13. The selection process for representatives to the National Assembly was on an unproportional basis. Moreover, of 37 parliamentary constituencies, an average of seven went under–represented each year in the 1970s (Mtewa, 1983).

14. Agricultural exports were highly concentrated: tobacco accounted for more than 60 per cent for most of the 1980s and 80 per cent in 1991, followed by tea, which accounted for about 20 per cent during the 1980s and only 8 per cent in 1991 (World Bank, 1995b).

15. The estimated Gini coefficient for smallholders, 0.20 for 1968–69, rose to 0.45 during 1984–85 (Pryor, 1990). The corresponding figure had risen to 0.57 in 1992, whereas the Gini coefficient for the whole of Malawi was 0.62 in 1992 (World Bank, 1995b).

16. In 1991 and 1992, the share of tobacco in total merchandise exports rose to more than 70 per cent (World Bank data files).

17. ADMARC was established in 1971 to replace the Farmers' Marketing Board of the colonial period.

18. With the worsening overall economic performance, ADMARC incurred large losses in 1980–81 and in 1986.

19. Between 1965 and 1973 there were only two nominal adjustments in wages: by less than 10 per cent in 1966 and by 5 per cent in 1973. Several major adjustments occurred between 1974 and 1992 — of 102 per cent in urban areas and 132 per cent in rural areas between 1980 and 1982, plus somewhat smaller ones in 1987, 1989 and 1992 — to keep both urban and rural real wages the same as in the 1970s.

20. The ratio of top to bottom civil–servant salaries fell from 40:1 in the 1970s to 32:1 in 1980, rose again to 46:1 in 1986, then fell to 25:1 in 1992.

21. The urban population in countries with similar income in sub–Saharan Africa was about 33 per cent in 1989 (World Bank, 1995a).

22. 35 per cent according to the Development Policy, 1986–96.

23. Average wages for unskilled workers were several times higher in South Africa than in Malawi during the decade after Malawi's Independence (World Bank, 1993*a*).

24. Commercial Bank of Malawi and National Bank of Malawi were established in 1970 and 1971, respectively.

25. An exception was the nationalisation of the railways in 1966.

26. Due to a limited manufacturing base, Malawi depended on imports for two–thirds of its intermediate goods and all of its capital goods (Kaluwa, 1992).

27. In 1985, small–scale manufacturing accounted for 30 per cent of total formal manufacturing employment (Pryor, 1990).

28. Debt service constituted less than 10 per cent of export earnings in 1977, but reached more than 30 per cent in 1981 and 1982 and more than 50 per cent in 1986, then fell to about 20 per cent in 1995 (see also Annex 2).

29. This ban came in reaction to a mining disaster that killed 75 Malawi miners. It is also argued that it might have aimed to obtain a better deal from South Africa for the migrant miners (Williams, 1978).

30. The British Government was a major source of military aid; Malawi covered only one–fifth of its military spending through its budget in 1971 (American University, 1985).

31. Per capita foreign disbursements in Malawi were about the same as the average for all developing countries, although slightly higher than for the poorest countries (Pryor, 1990).

32. Defined in US dollars.

33. The ratio of population in absolute poverty was 25 per cent in urban areas and 85 per cent in rural areas in 1985 (UNDP/World Bank, 1992).

34. Press Holding was the largest debtor in 1983 (Pryor, 1990).

35. Between 1970–75 and 1985–90, the death rate fell from 27 to 19 (per thousand), infant mortality fell from 191 to 152 (per thousand) and life expectancy rose from 41 to 48 years (World Bank, 1990*b*).

Chapter 7

Concluding Remarks

Although all the countries studied here belong to the same region and have colonial histories, they present a wide spectrum of political outcomes that range from severe conflict to stability. The analytical approach highlights the main historical, social and economic elements and the dynamic patterns within which they have affected political instability in each country. This study may help to improve the design of cross–sectional studies that mostly have used *ad hoc* political variables to explain differences in countries' development paths. It has aimed not only to contribute to the understanding and prediction of the political, social and economic development of the countries studied, but also to shed light on the analysis of political instability and its linkages with economic development in other parts of the world.

The Role of Culture and History

A country's political history and culture have immense implications for its socio–political stability. A history of armed struggle among identifiable groupings is likely to be associated with persistent political instability. In Zimbabwe, for example, the *Shona* and *Ndebele* groups had separate armies during the Independence struggle; in Mozambique, Independence came after ten years of conflict motivated by the FRELIMO objective of overthrowing the colonial power. Both of these countries' post–Independence periods also saw serious conflict. By contrast, Malawi had a generally peaceful tradition, influenced by the unifying role of the church prior to Independence, which accorded with a generally peaceful post–Independence period. Likewise, Botswana had neither an armed struggle for Independence nor a history of major conflict among groups, and these attributes played a major role in maintaining peace after Independence. Botswana's traditionally democratic institutions, which persisted, present an especially good example of the importance of a peaceful culture in maintaining political stability. Zambia represents more intermediary situations, in which post–Independence political instability appears in minor forms of tension between groups that emerge within inherited socio–economic structures.

Social and Economic Structures: Colonial Legacy and Post–Independence

The aggravation of political instability usually results from deepening inequity in asset distribution, or simply a perception of such inequity. Colonial regimes in southern Africa generally engaged in rent extraction from lands rich in natural resources or from particular economic activities. They thus established dual economic structures, where settlers often appropriated a substantial portion of the productive assets and the natives mostly did subsistence farming. After Independence, such economic structures usually gave way to the spread, or transfer, of inequality from between settlers and Africans to among newly emerging African groups. A post–Independence government's accommodative stance towards those who claim assets as compensation for their role in obtaining Independence may foster the emergence of such narrow groupings, even if at the expense of national objectives. The *Shona*, the largest ethnic group in Zimbabwe, and the unions in Zambia, originally established and empowered under the colonial economic structure, exemplify groups which, using the inherited economic structures, achieved both political and economic advantage over other groups after Independence.

Rapid changes of asset ownership — often from colonial administrations to Africans — are highly likely to lead to the emergence of such new groupings which, more often than not, would also like to maintain the prevailing economic structures. Maintaining such dual structures, in turn, may aggravate inequalities and thus the potential for political instability. Zambia, Zimbabwe, Mozambique and Malawi all realised large–scale nationalisations that amounted to the take–over of productive assets and the state machinery by their post–Independence governments. Such large–scale transfers, however, generally involve inadequately trained personnel and insufficient institutions; these conditions often open room for abuses of political power which in turn increase the potential for political instability.

Due to its apparent lack of natural resources, the colonial administration did not generate a large measure of duality in Botswana's economic structure. The relatively peaceful post–Independence period in this country resulted in part from this absence of dualism and in part from the Government's deliberate efforts to maintain it by avoiding discrimination both within the economic and political structures and in the extension of social services. Malawi, however, despite a highly dualistic economic structure, had relative political stability after Independence, due mainly to the Government's firm control over the formation of civil–society organisations.

Coincidence of Regional Boundaries and Occupations with Social Groupings

The attributes that make socio–economic groups politically powerful have great importance for identifying them in an analysis of political instability. A group will not contribute to instability unless it either has powerful means of expression or constitutes an identifiable political base. The potential for the organisation, and thus the impact, of such groups increases when occupational, ethnic or regional connections easily identify them. The internationally financed and trained RENAMO in Mozambique, the trade unions in Zambia and the *Shona* and *Ndebele* ethnic communities in Zimbabwe all provide examples of such groupings with an important impact on political instability. RENAMO had a powerful means of expression; the trade unions in Zambia had political power from their sectoral and regional concentration; and the *Shona* and the *Ndebele* represented regional ethnic concentrations. Ethnic diversity across regions and occupations in Botswana, Malawi and Zambia, on the other hand, gave relatively much less room for the formation of ethnically based political power centres than in Zimbabwe, for example, where ethnic groups were much more clearly divided by regional boundaries.

In many cases, ethnic groups may not have a history of conflict but may be provoked into it either through perceived or actual socio–economic discrimination, or through favouritism by political parties competing for power and prestige. Political developments in the countries studied here, including the democratic transitions since the late 1980s in Botswana, Malawi and Zambia, provide examples of this phenomenon, which generally occurs in reaction to increasing dissatisfaction with the government's performance.

The effect of groups' actions on political instability, however, normally relates directly to its net cost. If a group is small relative to the population and its asset claims are disproportionate to its size, its share of the net cost of the resulting asset redistribution may be smaller than the benefit it derives, notwithstanding that the net cost may involve increased potential for political instability. A relatively large group, on the other hand, may bear a large share of the net cost of redistribution or of disrupting the prevailing asset distribution. A sizeable and politically powerful group may therefore tend to avoid socio–economic discrimination that could provoke tension. This accords well with the generally observed positive relationship between political stability and economic development.

Economic Factors

The case studies support the general conclusion that when a nation's wealth shrinks, due either to economic mismanagement or to exogenous factors, the distributive or overall impact on the socio–economic structure becomes especially binding for political instability. In Mozambique, the post–Independence period, with its severe political conflict, also coincided with periods of floods (1974–76), droughts (1982–85 and 1991–92) and regional political instability that had dramatic economic consequences. In Zambia, following an economic boom and relative political stability, the potential for political instability increased with a fall in copper revenues and led to increased political opposition as the effects of the continued economic downturn affected increasingly larger groups in the population. In Zimbabwe, the Government's ability to control dissent through social–services spending was severely restrained by the fall in economic activity in 1982; the major outbreak of conflict also occurred that year. In Botswana, on the other hand, economic boom enabled the government to underscore the other elements of political stability by extending social services to larger groups of the population. In Malawi, relative political stability arose largely from successful economic management. Economic growth and good management of economic and financial resources thus appear to parallel a potential for political stability.

Policy Lessons

Historical, cultural and economic factors all affect the potential for political instability. While policy makers generally cannot change the course of exogenous events, the evolution of socio–economic structures and institutions does relate dynamically to government policies. Economic and political institutions have the ultimate role in averting political instability, because their policies govern how asset distribution — as broadly defined in this book — takes place. Notwithstanding an economy's accumulated imbalances and vulnerability to exogenous shocks, the policy response of the government to various forms of political opposition, whether in accommodation or repression, is more credible when it involves legal or administrative elements of institutional change. Any political or economic reform without sufficient attention to institutional restructuring is likely to fail.

The colonial and post–colonial examples of government emphasis on a single sector have been associated with highly concentrated power structures. In sub–Saharan Africa, many countries are land–locked, do not have diversified industries, and are largely agricultural. Political power usually coincides with estate ownership and commercial farming, leaving large parts of the population in subsistence agriculture in widely dispersed regions that frustrate the formation of interest–group organisations. While rent–seeking activities by narrow, politically powerful groups within such economic structures often paved the way for repressive acts in defence of the *status quo*, repressive policies eventually stimulated organised political opposition. Economic diversification improves the spread of political power *via* improved asset distribution. Economic reforms that target it through market mechanisms may thus improve the potential for political stability by preventing the concentration of economic and political power in the hands of a single group.

Economic reform programmes can nevertheless be potentially destabilising, for the following reasons. First, an attempt to redistribute assets in order to change apparently inefficient prevailing allocation and distribution patterns may increase potential political instability if it harms those who benefit from the existing patterns, and if they are organised and possess a means of expression. Radical reform programmes therefore often become very difficult in circumstances where an elite dominates the political and bureaucratic machinery, unless a major, organised political opposition supports the reforms. Second, especially in the absence of such support, when the economic and financial situation of a country necessitates reforms, institutional or other constraints may provoke political opposition and result in a government's loss of legitimacy. As various episodes of the countries studied here show, securing adequately trained personnel and establishing market institutions to attain good economic management, coupled with a transparent effort to accommodate rather than discriminate against various groups, help in large measure to achieve political stability. Political alignments with regional, ethnic and occupational groups, in contrast, may produce deep socio–economic divisions whose costs may surpass the benefits of such reforms.

Growth and equity objectives are often hard to achieve simultaneously, and the time horizon of the government, as well as the characteristics of groups it represents, play a large role in this trade–off. The extent of the trade–off also relates closely to the prevailing degree of economic disequilibrium, vulnerability to external shocks and the power of distributive coalitions. A government with a long horizon will likely target growth, possibly more than equity in the short term. By contrast, a government with a short horizon may completely discard the equity objective and engage in rent–seeking activities that may have long–term costs both for growth and in political instability. Institutional measures that ensure political stability and protect a democratic environment may give political parties a sense of continuity such that they care about the long–run costs and benefits of their economic policies.

Bibliography

ACDA (UNITED STATES ARMS CONTROL AND DISARMAMENT AGENCY) (1994/95), *World Military Expenditures and Arms Transfers*, Washington, D.C.

ADELMAN, I. and S. ROBINSON (1988), "Macroeconomic Adjustment and Income Distribution: Alternative Models Applied to Two Economies", *Journal of Development Economics*, 29:1, July.

AHLUWALIA, M.S. and H.B. CHENERY (1974), "The Economic Framework", in *Redistribution and Growth*, Oxford University Press, Oxford.

ALESINA, A., S. OZLER, N.R. and P. SWAGEL (1992), "Political Instability and Economic Growth", NBER Working Paper 4173, NBER, Cambridge, Mass.

ALESINA, A. and R. PEROTTI (1994), "The Political Economy of Growth: A Critical Survey of the Recent Literature", *World Bank Economic Review*, 8:3.

AMERICAN UNIVERSITY (1985), *A Country Study: Malawi*, Area Handbook Series, American University, Washington, D.C.

AZAM, J.–P. (1995), "Development Policy for Africa: A Research Agenda", in J.–C. Berthélemy, ed., *Whither Africa?*, OECD Development Centre, Paris.

BARDHAN, P. (1996), *The Role of Governance in Economic Development: A Political Economy Approach*, OECD Development Centre, Paris.

BARRO, R.J. (1996), "Determinants of Democracy", Harvard University, July, mimeo 7, Cambridge, Mass.

BARRO, R.J. (1991) "Economic Growth in a Cross–Section of Countries", *Quarterly Journal of Economics*, Vol. 106:2, May.

BECKMAN, B. (1991), "Empowerment or Repression? The World Bank and the Politics of African Adjustment", in *African Development*, Vol. XVI, No. 1.

BEN–HABIB, J. and M. SPIEGEL (1992), "The Role of Human Capital and Political Instability in Economic Development", *New York University Economic Research Reports*, 92:24, New York.

BRUTON, H.J. and C.B. HILL (eds.) (1996), *The Evaluation of Public Expenditure in Africa*, Economic Development Institute Learning Resources Series, World Bank, Washington, D.C.

CAMPBELL, B. and J. LOXLEY (1989), *Structural Adjustment in Africa*, Macmillan, London.

CODESRIA (1993), *Ethnic Conflict Report*, Dakar.

COLCLOUGH, C. (1980), *The Political Economy of Botswana*, Oxford University Press, Oxford.

DANEVAD, A. (1995), "Responsiveness in Botswana Politics: Do Elections Matter?", *The Journal of Modern African Studies*, 33:3.

DANEVAD, A. (1993), *Development Planning and the Importance of Democratic Institutions in Botswana*, Chr. Michelsen Institute, 1993:7.

DORNBUSCH, R. and S. EDWARDS (1990), "Macroeconomic Populism", *Journal of Development Economics*, Vol. 32, No. 1.

EASTERLY, W. and S. REBELO (1993), "Fiscal Policy and Growth: An Empirical Investigation", *Journal of Monetary Economics*, 32 (3).

FALLON, P.R. (1987), "The Labour Market in Zimbabwe: Historical Trends and an Evaluation of Recent Policy", DRD Discussion Paper 296, World Bank, Washington, D.C., May.

GERSONY, R. (1988), *Summary of Mozambican Refugee Accounts of Principally Conflict–Related Experience in Mozambique*, a study undertaken for the US Department of State, Washington, D.C.

GIBBONS, P. (1994), "Toward a Political Economy of the World Bank", in T. MKANDAWIRE and A. OLUKOSHI (eds), *Between Liberalism and Repression: The Politics of Adjustment in Africa*, CODESRIA, Dakar.

GOOD, K. (1994), "Corruption and Mismanagement in Botswana: A Best–Case Example?", *Journal of Modern African Studies*, 32:3.

GOVERNMENT OF BOTSWANA (1985), *The Development Policy, 1986–1996*, Gaberone.

GULHATI, R. (1989), *Malawi: Promising Reforms, Bad Luck*, EDI Development Policy Case Series, Analytical Case Studies, No. 3, World Bank, Washington, D.C.

HARVEY, C. and S.R. LEWIS (1990), *Policy Choice and Development Performance in Botswana*, St. Martin's Press, New York.

HIBBS, D. (1973), *Mass Political Violence: A Cross–Sectional Analysis*, Wiley, New York.

HOLM, J.D. and P.P. MOLUTSI (1992), "State–Society Relations in Botswana: Beginning Liberalization", in G. HYDEN and M. BRATTON (eds) *Governance and Politics*, London.

HOPE, K.R. (1995), "Managing Development Policy in Botswana: Implementing Reforms for Rapid Change", *Public Administration and Development*, Vol. 15.

HUNTINGTON, S. (1968), *Political Order in Changing Societies*, Yale University Press, New Haven, Conn.

ILO (1981), *An Economy Under Pressure*, ILO, Geneva.

KALUWA, B. (ed.) (1992), *The Structural Adjustment Programme in Malawi: A Case of Successful Adjustment?*, Sapes Books, Harare.

KANBUR, R. (1995), "A Continent in Transition: Sub–Saharan Africa in the Mid–1990s", mimeo, World Bank, Washington, D.C.

KYDD, J. and R. CHRISTIANSEN (1982), "Structural Change in Malawi Since Independence: Consequences of a Development Strategy Based on Large–Scale Agriculture", *World Development*, Vol. 10.

LELE, U. and L.R. MEYERS (1989), "Growth and Structural Change in East Africa: Domestic Policies, Agricultural Performance and World Bank Assistance, 1963–86", *Media Discussion Paper 3*, World Bank, Washington, D.C.

MADDISON, A. (1995), *Monitoring the World Economy, 1820–1992*, OECD Development Centre, Paris.

MAFEJE, A. (1995), "Demographic and Ethnic Variation: A Source of Instability in Modern African States", Paper presented to the CODESRIA 8th General Assembly.

MAMDANI, M. (1995), "Making Sense of the Political Impasse in Africa", Paper presented to the CODESRIA 8th General Assembly.

MANDAZA, I. (ed.) (1986), *The Political Economy of Transition: 1980–1986*, CODESRIA, Dakar.

M'BAYA, K. (1995), "The Economic Crisis, Adjustment and Democracy in Africa", in *Democratisation Processes in Africa*, CODESRIA, Dakar.

MEDIA DISCUSSION PAPER (1989), See LELE and MEYERS (1989).

MEISENDER, T. (1994), "Bonanza and Dependency in Botswana", *Studies in Comparative International Development*, Vol. 29, Spring.

MHONE, G.L.Z. (ed.) (1992), *Malawi at the Crossroads: The Post–Colonial Political Economy*, Sapes Books, Harare.

MKANDAWIRE, T. (1995a), "Beyond Crisis: Towards Democratic Developmental States in Africa", Paper presented to the CODESRIA 8th General Assembly.

MKANDAWIRE, T. (1995b), "Adjustment, Political Conditionality and Democratization in Africa", in *Democratisation Processes in Africa*, CODESRIA, Dakar.

MTEWA, M. (1983), *Malawi: Democratic Theory and Public Policy*, Schenkman Books, Inc., Cambridge, Mass.

NELSON, H.D. (ed.) (1984), *Mozambique: A Country Study*, Area Handbook Series, American University Press, Washington, D.C.

NNOLI, O. (1995), "Ethnic Conflicts and Democratization in Africa", Paper presented to the CODESRIA 8th General Assembly.

PARENTI, M. (1967), "Ethnic Politics and the Persistence of Ethnic Identification", *American Political Science Review*, Vol. LXI, No. 4.

PRYOR, F. (1990), *The Political Economy of Poverty, Equity and Growth: Malawi and Madagascar*, A World Bank Comparative Study, World Bank, Washington, D.C.

RAKNER, L. (1992), *Trade Unions in Processes of Democratisation. A Study of Party-Labour Relations in Zambia*, Chr. Michelsen Institute, Bergen.

ROTH (1994), "Land Tenure, Agrarian Structure, and Comparative Land Use Efficiency in Zimbabwe: Options for Land Tenure Reform and Land Redistribution", *Land Tenure Center Research Papers*, 117:1-182, University of Wisconsin–Madison.

SAHN, D.E. and J. ARULPRAGASAM (1991), "Development Through Dualism? Land Tenure, Policy, and Poverty in Malawi", Cornell Food and Nutrition Policy Program, Working Paper 9, Cornell University, Ithaca, NY.

SIPRI (1994), *Yearbook*, Stockholm, Almqvist and Wikseil.

TORDOFF, W. (1988), "Local Administration in Botswana", *Public Administration and Development*, Vol. 18.

UNDP/WORLD BANK (1992), *African Development Indicators*, World Bank, Washington, D.C.

VALENTINE, T.R. (1993), "Mineral–Led Economic Growth, Drought Relief and Incomes Policy", *American Journal of Economics and Sociology*, Vol. 52.

WILLIAMS, T.D. (1978), *Malawi: The Politics of Despair*, Cornell University Press, Ithaca, NY.

WORLD BANK (1995a), *Zimbabwe: Country Economic Memorandum*, Washington, D.C.

WORLD BANK (1995b), *Malawi Agricultural Sector Memorandum: Strategy Options in the 1990s*, Washington, D.C., March.

WORLD BANK (1995c), *Human Resources and Poverty: Profile and Priorities for Action*, Washington, D.C., November.

WORLD BANK (1993a), *The Labor Market and Wages Policy in Malawi*, report prepared for the Government of Malawi, Washington, D.C.

WORLD BANK (1993b), *Opportunities for Industrial Development in Botswana: An Economy in Transition*, Report No. 11267–BT, Washington, D.C.

WORLD BANK (1990a), *Mozambique: The Restoration of Rural Production and Trade*, Country Economic Memorandum, Washington, D.C.

WORLD BANK (1990b), *Growth Through Poverty Reduction*, Report No. 8140–MAI, Washington, D.C.

WORLD BANK (1989), *Sub–Saharan Africa: From Crisis to Sustainable Growth*, Washington, D.C.

WORLD BANK (1983), *Sub-Saharan Agriculture: Synthesis and Trade Prospects*, World Bank Staff Working Papers, No. 608, Washington, D.C.

OECD PUBLICATIONS, 2, rue André-Pascal, 75775 PARIS CEDEX 16
PRINTED IN FRANCE
(41 1999 11 1 P) ISBN 92-64-17164-9 – No. 51017 1999